100 GREATS

READING
FOOTBALL CLUB

Caricatures drawn for the local paper of the Reading team which began the 1926/27 season.

100 GREATS

READING
FOOTBALL CLUB

WRITTEN BY
DAVID DOWNS

TEMPUS

First published 2000
Copyright © David Downs, 2000

Tempus Publishing Limited
The Mill, Brimscombe Port,
Stroud, Gloucestershire, GL5 2QG

ISBN 0 7524 2081 X

Typesetting and origination by
Tempus Publishing Limited
Printed in Great Britain by
Midway Clark Printing, Wiltshire

Front cover : Skipper Keith McPherson holds aloft the Division Two
championship trophy which Reading won in 1993/94, supported by Shaka Hislop
and Mick Gooding.

Also available from Tempus Publishing

INTRODUCTION

One of the oldest and truest cliches in football is that the game is all about opinions. It follows therefore that the choice by any one supporter of the hundred greatest Reading Football Club players is unlikely to coincide exactly with the choice by any other. So my selection is an entirely personal one and of the great rather than the greatest of the 715 players who have represented the club in first-class matches.

Even so, there will be much opportunity for debate. Clearly, all those players who made three hundred or more appearances for Reading deserve to be included, and this group makes up one fifth of the selection. However, the choice of the remaining eighty will be more contentious. Arthur Bacon is there because he holds the record of scoring six goals for Reading in a Football League game. Johnny Brooks and Shaka Hislop had relatively short careers with Reading but went on to achieve fame and international recognition with other clubs. Others, like Fred Bartholomew, Gordon Neate, Roger Smee and Bobby Williams, merit inclusion not so much for their efforts on the pitch, but for the contribution they have made to the success of Reading FC off it. However, any player who has made one single first team appearance for the club has his own unique part in the history of the Reading Football Club and it may not be too long before another volume is compiled which contains details of every past and present Reading player.

I have been fortunate to watch the majority of the post-World War Two greats in action, whilst I know pre-war players only by reputation and much scrutiny of old scrapbooks and annuals. The statistics included with each of the biographies refer to games played since Reading entered the Football League Third Division in 1920.

I must explain the term 'Other competitions', used in the appearance records. The only 'other' pre-war competition was the Division Three (South) Cup, which Reading entered between 1933 and 1939, and which they won in 1937/38. Since World War Two, Reading have taken part in diverse competitions, including the Southern Professional Floodlit Cup, Watney Cup, Football League Group Cup, Football League Trophy, Associate Members' Cup, Division One play-off games and the Simod Cup. The latter competition provided the greatest single day in the club's long and distinguished history when, on Sunday 27 March 1988, Reading won the Simod Cup by defeating Luton Town 4-1 in the Wembley final. It is no coincidence that seven of the Reading players who were on duty that day are included in the One Hundred Greats.

ACKNOWLEDGEMENTS

I give my thanks to those people who have helped in the production of this book. Firstly, thanks to James Howarth of Tempus Publishing, who mooted the idea during the half-time interval of a Reading versus Plymouth Argyle FA Cup tie in December 1999. Besides providing the initial stimulus, James has offered much subsequent advice and support. Photographs and cartoons are drawn mainly from the club's own archive material, but I am also grateful to several people who have provided pictures, information and sometimes their own personal memories of players. These thoughtful people include Gary Arkell, Denis Barley, David Barr, Clive Baskerville, Leigh Edwards, Dave Goss, Bryan Horsnell, Gordon Page, Alan Sedunary, Roger Titford and Andy West. I also want to thank Marion for her patience in spending lonely hours in front of the television set while I have been researching and writing this book. Final thanks must go to all the players, chairmen, directors, managers and other officials of Reading Football Club whose dedication and wonderful deeds have actually made a book of this nature possible.

Up the Royals!

David Downs
November 2000

Syd Jordan drew these sketches of the team which began the 1950/51 season, for the Reading Standard.

100 READING GREATS

Denis Allen
Bill Amor
Sylvan Anderton
Philip Bach
Arthur Bacon
Joe Bailey
Charlie Barley
Fred Bartholomew
Stuart Beavon
Ron Blackman
Richie Bowman
Teddy Braithwaite
Kevin Bremner
Gordon Brice
Johnny Brooks
Matt Busby
Billy Butler
Dennis Butler
Bobby Campbell
Bryan Carnaby
Darren Caskey
Les Chappell
Alec Christie
Syd Crawford
Gordon Cumming
Hugh Davey
Bill Davies
Steve Death
Kerry Dixon
Mike Dixon
Tommy Dixon
Joe Duckworth
Pat Earles
Maurice Edelston

Bert Eggo
David Evans
Maurice Evans
Alan Foster
Steve Francis
Robin Friday
Michael Gilkes
Gilbert Glidden
Mick Gooding
Len Grant
Dick Habbin
Ted Hanney
George Harris
Albert Hayhurst
Stanley Hayward
Stewart Henderson
Les Henley
Steve Hetzke
Martin Hicks
Shaka Hislop
Johnny Holt
Dean Horrix
George Johnson
David Jones
Mike Kearney
Jack Lewis
Stuart Lovell
Magnus MacPhee
George Marks
Billy McConnell
Mark McGhee
Joe McGough
Keith McPherson
Colin Meldrum

Alf Messer
Gordon Neate
Jack Palethorpe
Phil Parkinson
Gary Peters
Jimmy Quinn
Ray Reeves
Frank Richardson
Steve Richardson
Lawrie Sanchez
Trevor Senior
Roger Smee
Herbert Smith
Dick Spiers
Tommy Tait
Scott Taylor
Pat Terry
Barry Wagstaff
Johnny Walker
Jimmy Wallbanks
Dougie Webb
Neil Webb
Jimmy Wheeler
Mark White
Percy Whittaker
Stan Wicks
Arthur Wilkie
Adrian Williams
Bobby Williams
Jerry Williams
Steve Wood
Tommy Youlden

The top twenty players appear here in italics. Each of these particuarly great Reading stars are allocated two pages instead of the usual one.

Denis Allen

Utility player, 1961-1970

	First Team Appearances	Goals
Football League	335	84
FA Cup	24	6
FL Cup	18	5
Other	0	0
TOTAL	377	94

A member of the famous footballing Allen family from Dagenham, Denis joined Charlton Athletic on leaving school and made a total of 5 first team appearances for the Valley club before joining Reading in 1961. His career at Charlton had been interrupted by National Service, during which he had been posted to Malaya – where he achieved the rare distinction of representing that country twice in international matches.

Allen cost Reading just £900, but proved to be one of manager Harry Johnston's shrewdest investments. He was to stay for ten years, play over 300 first team games and score almost 100 goals. He could also fill any position, beginning his career at Elm Park in the forward line (where he performed equally well on the wing, at inside forward or centre forward), before dropping back into midfield and finally spending his last season as a centre-back. Furthermore, he took over as the emergency goalkeeper in two games where the regular 'keeper had been injured.

He was a tricky, artful and entertaining player and popular with the fans. He marked his 300th League game for Reading, against Bournemouth on 20 September 1969, in a typically flamboyant fashion: Reading won 2-0, Allen scoring both goals from long-range direct free kicks.

It was something of a surprise when Allen, who had been club captain during the 1969/70 season, joined Bournemouth in the summer. He stayed with the South Coast club for a year, returning to Elm Park to enjoy a well-deserved testimonial against an All-Star XI, then took over as player-manager at Cheltenham Town in the Southern League. After several successful seasons there he became a director of Exeter City Football Club, and also ran coaching courses for the Football Association. His playing career ended with appearances in charity and exhibition games, and he also played for a local Reading Sunday team, the Beetle & Wedge FC.

Sadly, Denis died in 1995, but not before he had seen his son Martin play for West Ham United in the Premier League. Denis would have been proud to know that Martin joined Reading FC as assistant manager in January 2000.

Denis Allen challenges the Gillingham goalkeeper for a near-post cross.

	First Team Appearances	Goals
Football League	66	12
FA Cup	2	0
FL Cup	0	0
Other	0	0
TOTAL	68	12

Amateur players were a rarity in League teams even in the days immediately after the Second World War, but Reading regularly fielded two in their forward line. One was Maurice Edelston, already an amateur international, and the other was Bill Amor. Reading had tried several players at outside left in the 1947/48 season, none of whom were consistently successful. In desperation the club turned to Amor, a constable in the Reading Borough Police, who was playing at the time for Huntley & Palmers FC in the Spartan League, as well as Reading Reserves. He made his debut against Ipswich Town on 14 February 1948, and the *Berkshire Chronicle* reported on his 'brilliant passing'.

Amor soon attracted the attention of the England amateur selectors, and when he scored a hat-trick in the FA XI's 4-0 victory over the Scottish side Queen's Park, his international selection seemed assured. There were formalities to be completed, and Reading secretary Fred May received a request from FA secretary Stanley Rous enquiring whether PC Amor would be available to play for England. Mr May rang Jesse Lawrence, Reading Chief Constable, permission was granted, and Amor was capped for England against Wales at Shrewsbury. A further honour came his way when he was included in the Great Britain Olympic squad for the 1948 games in London. He played at left-wing for the team which lost 3-5 to Denmark in the play-off match for third and fourth place in the tournament.

Bill, whose amateur status was denoted by the initials before his name in match programmes, made intermittent appearances for the Biscuitmen over five seasons, totalling 68 first team games and scoring 12 goals. He was a powerful, thrusting winger, with the pace to round his full-back and deliver an accurate centre, but who could also cut in and hammer a thunderous shot to the far post, or rise to head in a centre from the opposite flank. He always wore the number eleven shirt in his first team games. Revealing his versatility, in 1951 Police Constable Amor won the one-mile bicycle race in uniform at the police sports day held at Simonds Sports Ground in Berkeley Avenue.

Popular as a footballer and as a policemen, Bill served in the Reading Borough and then Thames Valley Police forces until he retired in 1975. A regular churchgoer and keen gardener, he lived in Reading until his death in 1988.

Sylvan Anderton

Wing-half, 1952-1959

S. ANDERTON *(Reading)*

	First Team Appearances	Goals
Football League	155	18
FA Cup	12	1
FL Cup	0	0
Other	11	0
TOTAL	178	19

One of the most exciting products of the youth development scheme instituted by manager Ted Drake in the early 1950s was Sylvan Anderton, an elegant and stylish wing-half who began his playing career in local football with Battle Athletic.

He made his debut for Reading in the 'B' team, which won Division Two of the Reading & District League during the 1951/52 season, and went on to score 43 goals in just 25 appearances. Clearly he was destined for greater things, and steady progress through the 'A' and reserve teams followed until he made his first team debut against Leyton Orient in a 1-1 draw the following season. He was just eighteen, and National Service restricted his first team football for the next couple of years. Once established in the side, however, he kept his place. His clever and thoughtful play was not always appreciated in the hurly-burly of Third Division football, and he was constantly moved from his original position of wing-half to inside forward and back again. But he never complained, and got on with the job of serving to the best of his ability the home town team which gave him his chance in League football.

Anderton made almost 200 first team appearances, and scored 19 first team goals, the best of which was a long-distance strike which brought a 1-0 victory over Bournemouth in an FA Cup first round tie in November 1955. It was inevitable that a First Division club would eventually sign a player of such class, and he was transferred to Chelsea for a fee of £10,000 in March 1959, having spent eight years at Reading. He was with the Stamford Bridge club for a little over three seasons, mostly in the senior team, with a total of 82 games and 2 goals. He had added steel to his play since leaving Elm Park, and became popular with the discerning Chelsea crowd as a hard-tackling, yet constructive half-back. In January 1962 he made one more move, joining Queens Park Rangers, then in Division Three, and making 4 appearances before dropping out of League football at the end of the season. Sylvan now lives in Bideford, North Devon, where he writes poetry and also scouts for Reading.

Philip Bach
Full-back, 1895-1897

	First Team Appearances	Goals
Football League	0	0
FA Cup	5	0
FL Cup	0	0
Other	0	0
TOTAL	5	0

When Reading Football Club decided to adopt professionalism in 1895, the committee began to cast around for players of potential rather than experience, as funds were limited. One of the best young players to join the club during the close season of that year was Philip Bach, a twenty-two-year-old defender signed from Middlesborough. He was immediately appointed as captain, a position he held throughout the Southern League campaign of 1895/96, when Reading finished in fourth place out of the ten teams in Division One. Although he failed to score, he was described as a 'useful full-back and a model of consistency, sound rather than brilliant.'

He remained with Reading for one more season and also captained the team which played in the opening fixture at Elm Park, when Reading beat Mr A. Roston Bourke's London XI by seven goals to nil. Reading dropped to sixth position at the end of the 1896/97 season and during the summer Bach was transferred to Sunderland, then in Division One of the Football League. He remained at Sunderland for three seasons and during that time won his only England international cap, when he was selected at right-back for the team which set a record by beating Ireland 13-2 at Roker Park. One year later he was on the move to Bristol City, where he stayed until 1904 before being reinstated as an amateur.

Bach now began a thirty-year career as a leading administrator in the game. He returned to the North-East and was elected as a Middlesborough director in 1911. He became chairman of the club in the same year and held that post until 1925. He was re-appointed as chairman in 1931 and finally resigned in 1935. He was an FA Councillor from 1925 to 1937 and a member of the FA Selection Committee, who were responsible for picking the England team, from October 1929. He was also on the Football League Management Committee from 1929 until his death on 30 December 1937. Throughout his time in these posts, he had carried on his trade as proprietor of the Empire Hotel in Middlesborough.

Thus, although Philip Bach spent just two full seasons with Reading Football Club, he deserves his place in the history of the club not only for his career on the field, but for the considerable part he played in the development of the national sport.

Arthur Bacon
Centre forward, 1929-1932

	First Team Appearances	Goals
Football League	69	44
FA Cup	4	1
FL Cup	0	0
Other	0	0
TOTAL	73	45

Arthur Bacon was signed by Reading from Manchester City in October 1929, to replace the free-scoring Frank Richardson – something he did to consummate effect. In his first season he scored just 3 goals in 13 games, but the following season totalled 30 from 35 first team games. He was not the most skilful player ever seen in a Reading shirt, but was renowned for having a powerful shot in both feet. Once he sent a shot out of the ground, which smashed a gas bracket in a house in Kent Road. His surname gave rise to many witty remarks, including a shout from the crowd at a reserve game of 'You and two eggs would make a fine breakfast.' A great admirer of Bacon was John Arlott, who described him as 'A tall man with a shaving-brush tuft of hair growing out from a shallow forehead above a mighty jaw. His chest was like a drum, his thighs hugely tapering and he had two shooting feet which he threw at footballs as if with intent to burst them.'

Bacon's scoring record in 1930/31 was all the more remarkable as Reading were relegated from Division Two that season, but not before Bacon had established an individual landmark which still stands to this day. On 3 April 1931, Reading defeated Stoke City 7-3 at Elm Park, with Bacon scoring six of the goals and Barley the seventh. Bacon played the kind of game that centre forwards dream about. It seemed that every time he shot, the ball flew at the Stoke goal like a bullet. His last goal was the most remarkable, as he shot from what seemed an impossibly acute angle, but still smashed the ball high into the roof of the net.

Bacon joined Chesterfield in 1932 and a year later moved to Coventry City. In a five-match spell in late 1933 Bacon scored fifteen goals, but spent most of his time at the Midland club with the reserve team in the London Combination. From 1937 until the outbreak of war he played non-League football for Burton Town. He returned to Derby to live and was killed in an air raid on the town in January 1941, when he fell off his bicycle while serving as a special constable.

Only Ron Blackman, who twice scored 5 goals in a game, has come close to equalling Bacon's record, which seems likely to last forever.

	First Team Appearances	Goals
Football League	41	17
FA Cup	15	5
FL Cup	0	0
Other	0	0
TOTAL	56	22

A regular at inside-left in the Reading team which played in the Southern League in the seasons before the First World War was W.G. Bailey, popularly known as Joe or 'Bubbles' Bailey. Born at Thame in 1890, he was an amateur in a team consisting mainly of professionals. His ability was such that he was selected for the England amateur team which played against both Belgium and Holland in the 1912/13 season, scoring twice in each game. The outbreak of war interrupted his football career and he volunteered for the Footballers' Battalion of the Middlesex Regiment, where he served with distinction. He was commissioned, rose to the rank of Captain, and was decorated for bravery, winning the Distinguished Service Order and Military Cross with two bars.

He rejoined Reading FC at the end of hostilities and played in the club's first-ever Football League match, away to Newport County in a Third Division fixture on Saturday 28 August 1920. After twenty-eight minutes' play, Reading scored the only goal of the game. Left-winger Andrews beat his full-back out on the touchline, sent over a pinpoint centre, and Bailey 'guided the ball delicately out of the goalkeeper's reach.'

However, Bailey will be remembered for more than becoming Reading's first Football League goalscorer. He was also the leading scorer for the season, netting 17 goals in 41 League matches. In March 1921 he had one of his best games, completing a hat-trick as Northampton Town were beaten 4-0. He may have been inspired by the fact that on the train journey back from the Northampton away fixture the previous week, the Reading team had been introduced to the Prince of Wales, who bought tickets for Bailey's benefit match against Plymouth Argyle. That game was played in April and brought Bailey the handsome sum of £326, more than enough to buy a small house.

Bailey was an excellent all-round sportsman. He represented Oxfordshire at hockey, was a qualified referee and played cricket for Berkshire between 1911 and 1920. At the end of the 1920/21 season, he left Elm Park to become cricket coach at Warwick School. In later life he moved to Weymouth and he died in the South Coast town in 1974.

Charlie Barley
Left half, 1929-1937

	First Team Appearances	Goals
Football League	194	16
FA Cup	19	0
FL Cup	0	0
Other	1	0
TOTAL	214	16

Charlie Barley began his working life as a Derbyshire coal miner, but he was spotted playing amateur football by legendary Arsenal manager Herbert Chapman and signed for the Gunners in 1927. Although he made only 10 first team appearances, scoring once, he did win three Football Combination championship medals with Arsenal Reserves, in consecutive seasons from 1926/27 to 1928/29.

With limited opportunities at Highbury, Barley moved to Reading in exchange for Bill Johnstone in May 1929 and became a first team regular at Elm Park for the next four seasons. He played mostly at left half, sometimes at inside-left, and occasionally at centre half or left-back. In each position his play was characterised by a dynamic mixture of aggression and skill. He employed a hard, decisive tackle and, although his temperament was slightly suspect, his prompting from the half-back line was extremely useful to forwards. He was an effective long-range marksman too and could be relied on for a handful of goals each season.

One of his loyal young supporters in the 1930s was Michael Bond (author of the Paddington Bear books), who spent his childhood in Reading. Bond recalls meeting Barley while the footballer was pushing his bicycle up the steep hill on Cranbury Road. He plucked up the courage to begin a conversation with his idol, but was surprised to find him out of breath!

Barley was a keen card player, golfer and part-time salesman who would bring a suitcase full of clothing to show to the other players each Friday, which was payday. His playing appearances declined as the years went by, and he was given a free transfer in 1937. He joined Maidenhead United as trainer/coach and groundsman, and played a few matches for the Magpies. But it did not last, because he said the players were too old to accept his innovative coaching methods.

During the Second World War, Barley served as a War Reserve Constable, ensuring the blackout regulations were adhered to in Reading, and played his last games of football for police teams. After the war, he opened a shop in the Basingstoke Road, which dealt in haberdashery, hairdressing and hardware.

Charlie Barley had two sons; Derek was an Arsenal junior and England Youth international in 1950, while Denis played for Thorneycrofts FC and in local football, frequently appearing alongside Maurice Edelston for the Shop Assistants XI that competed in the Reading Wednesday League.

Fred Bartholomew
Utility player, 1904-1921

	First Team Appearances	Goals
Football League	8	0
FA Cup	14	0
FL Cup	0	0
Other	0	0
TOTAL	22	0

The record for the longest period of service to Reading FC belongs to Fred Bartholemew. He was born in Reading in 1884 and was a prominent local footballer in his youth, playing for the Reading Biscuit Factory team, whom he assisted in winning the Berks & Bucks Junior Cup, Reading Town Cup and Tilehurst Charity Cup.

He soon came to the attention of Reading and signed for the Elm Park club as an amateur on Good Friday 1904, turning professional three years later.

Bartholomew played for Reading as a regular member of the Southern League team, except for the First World War period when he joined the Footballers' Battalion under the command of Major Buckley, and reached the rank of Company Quartermaster Sergeant.

After demobilisation he rejoined Reading and, at the age of thirty-seven, made eight appearances for the first team in its first season in the Football League Division Three in 1920/21. His testimonial match against Millwall in 1910 raised £17, mostly in farthings.

During his playing career he filled every position including that of goalkeeper and when his days on the field came to an end he took on the role of assistant trainer for three seasons. Even when that stint came to an end he continued to serve the club and became groundsman.

Working on the pitch in those days was hard, backbreaking labour, but 'Old Bart' as he was now affectionately known, kept his horse in a horse-box on the Tilehurst Road side of the ground. The animal was used to pull the heavy roller around the pitch, but the biggest cheers were reserved for Old Bart when, single-handed, he would remove the tarpaulins from the goalmouth before the start of a game on a waterlogged surface.

Old Bart continued as groundsman until 1957 when he finally retired after fifty-three years with Reading FC. Even then he remained a loyal supporter of the team, making the short journey from his home just off the Oxford Road to Elm Park until well into his eighties.

Stuart Beavon

Midfielder, 1980-1990

	First Team Appearances	Goals
Football League	396	44
FA Cup	32	3
FL Cup	28	2
Other	25	6
TOTAL	481	55

Although he went to school in Oxford, Stuart Beavon joined Tottenham Hotspur as an apprentice at the age of sixteen, then signed as a professional for the London club in July 1976. First team opportunities were limited, so he went on loan to Notts County, where he added 6 Football League games to the 3 he had played for Spurs.

He joined Reading for £35,000 in July 1980, making his debut in a 2-0 home win over Walsall, and for the next decade was virtually ever-present in midfield. He was an outstanding ball-passer, creating a constant supply of chances for the strikers, but he could also weigh in with goals of his own. He added strength and tenacity to his exquisite skills once Ian Branfoot arrived as manager and played a vital role in the team which ran away with the Division Three title in 1985/86. In 1987/88 he played in all six matches in the Simod Cup, which Reading won, converting vital penalty kicks in the semi-final shootout against Coventry City and putting Reading 2-1 ahead from the spot in the Wembley final against Luton Town. The following season he was a member of the side which narrowly avoided relegation from Division Three, and totalled 10 goals – this was the only campaign in which he reached double figures. Seven of those were penalties, including two in the 4-2 away win over Chesterfield on the last day of the season. That was a game Reading needed to win to stay up and Beavon's accuracy from the twelve-yard mark was a vital factor in enabling the club to do so.

Stuart left Reading in the 1990 close season and moved to Northampton Town as joint player-manager. He had always been popular with Reading fans and it was no surprise that he returned to the town after 98 League games and 14 goals for the Cobblers. He combined playing part-time football for Newbury Town, then Kintbury, with his trade as a painter and decorator, and has most recently been appearing in the colours of Reading Town on Saturdays and Abbey Whitchurch on Sundays. He always turns out for an ex-Reading XI in charity games and has on occasions played in the same Reading Town team as his son, Stuart junior.

He is one of only eight players to have completed over 400 first team appearances for Reading, and was awarded a well-deserved testimonial game in 1991.

Beavon follows up to score the first Reading goal in a 3-0 home win against Port Vale on 1 April 1989.

t Beavon celebrates with Kevin Bremner after the pair had scored the goals which beat Newport County 2-0 on 1.
ber 1985.

Ron Blackman

Centre forward, 1946-1954

	First Team Appearances	Goals
Football League	228	158
FA Cup	12	9
FL Cup	0	0
Other	0	0
TOTAL	**240**	**167**

Any selection of an all-time Reading XI would include Ron Blackman at centre forward as he is considered to be the most prolific goalscorer in the club's history. Born in Cosham in 1925, he was spotted playing for Gosport Borough and joined Reading as a part-timer in February 1947. He played mainly in the Hampshire League and Football Combination teams until 12 February 1949, when he was selected at the last minute for the Football League match at home to Leyton Orient and scored a hat-trick in Reading's 3-0 win. He signed as a full professional in August that year and took over from the ageing Tony MacPhee as the regular centre forward. He developed into the best goalscorer in the lower divisions and in both 1950/51 and 1951/52 totalled 40 League and cup goals, as Reading went close to gaining promotion from Division Three (South). His 39 League goals in 1951/52 still stand as a club record and seem unlikely ever to be beaten. Although he had a powerful shot in both feet,

his main asset was his lethal heading ability and the majority of his goals came from beautifully directed headers, mainly resulting from accurate crosses by wingers Simpson and Bainbridge.

Blackman's clashes with some of the Third Division (South)'s centre halves were not for the faint hearted, though despite his strong build Blackman was a gentleman on and off the pitch. He could seemingly score at will against lesser opposition and his exploits led to Second Division Nottingham Forest buying him for £8,000 in the 1954 close season. Although Blackman did not wish to move, especially as the maximum wage was still in operation and he was settled in Reading, the fee solved the club's financial problems. He was never the same player at Forest and subsequently moved on to Ipswich, where he stayed for three seasons. He then left full-time football, signed for Tonbridge and took up a career with the Post Office.

Still remembered with great affection by those who were lucky enough to see him play, Ron frequently returns to Reading to attend players' reunions and keeps in touch with many of the friends he made in the town. Now living quietly in retirement in Fareham, he made one last nostalgic visit to Elm Park in September 1998 before the ground was demolished.

Blackman scores Reading's first goal in the 2-0 win against Colchester United on 3 September 1952.

Blackman, third from left, back row, pictured in a Reading team group at the start of the 1952/53 season.

Richie Bowman
Midfielder, 1976-1981

	First Team Appearances	Goals
Football League	195	30
FA Cup	11	1
FL Cup	17	1
Other	0	0
TOTAL	223	32

Richie Bowman was born in London and joined his local club, Charlton, straight from school. He became a regular in the first team but was signed by Reading manager Maurice Evans for the amazingly low fee of £8,000 in December 1976. He immediately established himself in the Royals' midfield and, despite his slight stature, could always be found where the battle was fiercest, blocking shots with his body in his own penalty area one minute, then diving to head the ball towards the opponents' goal the next.

He was elected as the supporters' Player of the Season for 1977/78 and 1978/79 and in the latter season was also chosen for the PFA Division Four team. He was captain of the side which won the Division Four championship in 1978/79 and did not miss a game until injured by a dreadful tackle in a home game against Hartlepool.

He scored more than his fair share of goals from midfield, including some clinically taken penalties. Defensively he was coolness itself, even under the severest pressure, contributing significantly to the run of games in 1979 when Reading set a Football League record (which still stands) by not conceding a goal for eleven consecutive matches.

Described by manager Evans as the best professional he worked with during his time at the club, Bowman stayed for two more seasons after promotion into Division Three. He was consistent and reliable, missing only one first team game in 1979/80, and just two in 1980/81. By the time he left Elm Park he had made a total of 223 appearances and scored 32 goals.

He failed to agree terms with Reading in the summer of 1981 and eventually moved to Gillingham for a fee of £25,000, set by a Football League tribunal. A succession of niggling injuries curtailed his career with the Kent club, and he retired from playing in 1984. Lately, he has been running a sandwich bar in London.

He visited the Madejski Stadium in October 2000 to make the half-time Golden Gamble lottery draw for promotions manager Mike Kearney, his former playing colleague.

	First Team Appearances	Goals
Football League	133	22
FA Cup	17	4
FL Cup	0	0
Other	0	0
TOTAL	150	26

Teddy Braithwaite was born in Salford in 1902 and played for New Cross before signing for Bradford City in 1922. He made only 18 first team appearances for the Yorkshire club, scoring once, before moving south to join Reading in July 1924.

Braithwaite spent four very successful seasons at Elm Park. He began as a right-winger, but soon moved to inside forward, where his intuitive passing created many openings for other players. In 1924/25 he scored 6 times in 38 matches.

He realised his full potential in the Division Three (South) championship-winning side of 1925/26. He was one of only three always present in the team – Duckworth and Messer were the others – and got the campaign off to a flying start by scoring the first goal in the 3-2 defeat of Exeter City at Elm Park in the opening game.

He remained a regular in the side the following season, 1926/27 as Reading fought to establish themselves in the Second Division and also played in all the FA Cup ties up to and including round six, where he gave a superb display in the 3-1 away victory over Swansea Town. He missed the semi-final against Cardiff City through injury, however, and his absence contributed greatly to Reading's defeat.

Braithwaite stayed at Reading for two further seasons, but was no longer assured of a permanent place in the team. He did not enjoy reserve football, and in the close season of 1929 moved yet again, this time to Swindon Town, which became his final professional club. Towards the end of his life he moved to Kent and died there in 1990.

Braithwaite will be remembered as a vital and reliable member of the Reading team which set several records. These were: best performance in the FA Cup, highest League position (at the time) of fourteenth in Division Two and also the club's (then) record League victory, which came on 16 October 1926 when Reading defeated Notts County 7-1, with Braithwaite scoring twice.

Kevin Bremner

Forward, 1985-1987

	First Team Appearances	Goals
Football League	64	21
FA Cup	6	0
FL Cup	4	1
Other	2	0
TOTAL	76	22

Kevin Bremner signed for Reading for £30,000 from Millwall at the start of the 1985/86 season. Although he only spent two years with the club, they coincided with one of the most exciting spells in the history of Elm Park.

Bremner arrived to complement the already established strike force of Trevor Senior and Dean Horrix, but such was his form in pre-season friendlies that he forced his way into the team for the opening match of the campaign at home to Blackpool. Reading won that game 1-0, but Bremner was taken off before half-time with sprained knee ligaments and did not return to the side until six games later. Reading had won those six games and went on to set a Football League record (which still stands) by winning their first twelve League matches of the season. In the twelfth game, away to Newport County, Reading were desperately holding on to a 1-0 lead when Bremner was introduced as substitute and scored a second goal for the Royals with a superb diving header from Stuart Beavon's cross.

His best performance of the Division Three championship season came in the 4-3 home win over promotion rivals Plymouth Argyle. Reading were losing 0-3 soon after the interval when Bremner took the game by the scruff of the neck. He made three Reading goals, then scored the winner himself six minutes from time. That game exemplified the bravery and doggedness that so endeared him to Reading fans during his time at the club.

Bremner played in every game of the following season, 1986/87, as Reading sought to establish themselves as a Second Division side, scoring 16 goals in 47 appearances. He had proved the perfect partner for Senior, but left at the end of that season to join Brighton & Hove Albion for £65,000. He later returned to his native Scotland to play in junior football, but has most recently been working as youth team manager at Gillingham FC. His enthusiasm for the game remains undiminished and he even played one game in goal for Gillingham Reserves when the nominated 'keeper was delayed by a traffic jam.

	First Team Appearances	Goals
Football League	198	9
FA Cup	12	1
FL Cup	0	0
Other	0	0
TOTAL	210	10

Service in the Commando forces during World War Two prepared Gordon Brice admirably for the rigours of professional football, and he made League appearances for Luton Town and Wolverhampton Wanderers before joining Reading in March 1948.

He made an immediate debut for the reserve team which beat Spurs in the semi-final of the Combination Cup, playing in borrowed boots and finishing with both feet covered in blisters. Once he had won his place at centre half in the first team he was there to stay and established a club record of 147 consecutive first team appearances from the beginning of the 1948/49 season.

Generally agreed to be one of the best, if not the best centre half in the lower divisions, Brice was a tough but classy defender, able to win the ball with apparently consummate ease, either on the ground or in the air. On several occasions he had to mark Tommy Lawton, then playing for Notts County, and never allowed the England international to get the better of him.

Brice had other talents besides football. During the summer months he played county cricket for Northamptonshire and was a medium fast bowler of some note.

Cricketing activities always had to be curtailed, however, when he reported for pre-season training at Elm Park.

He also managed a sports shop in Reading, which was opened by Ted Drake and John Arlott in 1951, in partnership with Maurice Edelston,. He diversified on the football pitch too and at the start of the 1950/51 campaign played ten games at centre forward for Reading, scoring three goals.

Brice left Reading in December 1952 to join Fulham, where he stayed for two and a half seasons and made a further 87 League appearances. He later moved to Bedford to live, occasionally returning to Elm Park to watch the club which he had served so well.

Johnny Brooks
Inside forward, 1949-1953

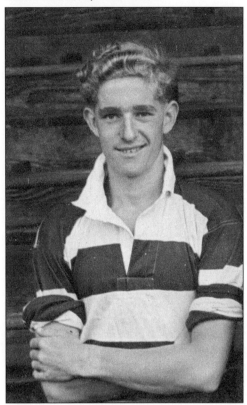

	First Team Appearances	Goals
Football League	46	5
FA Cup	3	1
FL Cup	0	0
Other	0	0
TOTAL	49	6

Reading-born Johnny Brooks began his football career with Coley Boys Club, joined Reading as a seventeen-year-old amateur in 1949 and made his debut for the first team whilst on National Service with the Army Catering Corps based in Aldershot. It soon became apparent that he was a most gifted inside forward, with outstanding ball control and the ability to spray passes with perceptive accuracy all over the pitch.

After only 49 first team games and 6 goals he was transferred to First Division Tottenham Hotspur in exchange for two players, Harry Robshaw and Dennis Uphill, plus a fee of £10,000. He made his first appearance for the London club in February 1953 and stayed for six seasons, earning a reputation as one of the most skilful players of his day. He played three times for England, scoring in his first two games for the national team against Wales and Yugoslavia.

In 1959 he moved to Chelsea, but was not able to repeat the success he had enjoyed at White Hart Lane and two years later he moved again. This time he signed for Brentford, and with that club won a Division Four championship medal in 1963. The following year he moved to yet another London club, Crystal Palace, before crossing the Atlantic for a brief but successful and enjoyable spell with Toronto in the Canadian League.

He returned to England and retired from full-time football, but combined playing for non-League Stevenage with a job as a messenger at the Stock Exchange in London. His son Shaun became an England schoolboy international, then played for Crystal Palace and Orient. Johnny meanwhile kept himself fit by frequently returning to Reading to play in friendly and charity matches.

As the first Reading-born player to be selected for England, it was fitting that he played in the final match to be staged at Elm Park – a veterans' tournament on 25 September 1998. Now living in Bournemouth, John is still an occasional visitor to the Madejski Stadium.

Matt Busby

Right half, 1942-1945

	First Team Appearances	Goals
Football League	0	0
FA Cup	0	0
FL Cup	0	0
Other (wartime)	40	0
TOTAL	40	0

Although Matt Busby never made a Football League appearance for Reading, he deserves to be included in any register of celebrated former players of the club. He did represent Reading in wartime football and went on to become probably the best-known postwar British club manager. Busby always retained an affinity for Reading, which became apparent on several occasions.

Before the outbreak of war, Busby had been playing for Liverpool and Manchester City and won one cap for Scotland. During hostilities he was stationed at Aldershot as an instructor with the Army Physical Training Corps and, in common with many other professional footballers, made guest appearances for a number of clubs.

He made his debut for Reading in a 0-0 home draw against Aldershot on 9 May 1942 and before the end of the war had made a total of 40 appearances, mostly at right-half. His final game was at home to Crystal Palace on 19 September 1945, when it was known that he was about to be appointed as manager of Manchester United. Reading made him captain for the occasion and held a leaving party for him after the game.

Busby returned to Elm Park in 1951 when he brought the full Manchester United team to play in a benefit match for two home players, Freddie Fisher and Jeff Gulliver. The two teams competed at golf on the afternoon of the match and the first prize of a clock was presented to Busby as a souvenir of the occasion.

He also came back to the ground in January 1955, when Reading held United to a 1-1 draw in an FA Cup tie before losing the replay at Old Trafford. Busby was reputedly the happiest man in Reading at the conclusion of the first game, because United only equalised just before full time.

Matt Busby survived the Munich air disaster of 1958 and led Manchester United to triumphs in the Football League, FA Cup and European Cup. He was knighted for his services to football and will always be regarded as one of the greatest figures in the history of the game.

Billy Butler
Winger, 1933-1935

	First Team Appearances	Goals
Football League	56	13
FA Cup	8	3
FL Cup	0	0
Other	2	0
TOTAL	66	16

Billy Butler had never played organised football before he joined the Army during the First World War, but he learnt enough during service with the Royal North Lancashire Regiment to be signed by Atherton, his home town club, on demobilisation. From there he joined First Division Bolton Wanderers and became one of the outstanding wingers of his day. He won an England cap against Scotland in 1924 and three FA Cup winner's medals with Bolton, in 1923, 1926, and 1929 (when he scored in the final against Portsmouth). Butler went on the transfer list at his own request when Bolton were relegated to Division Two in 1933 and stepped down a further division when he was reunited with his former team-mate, Joe Smith, who was by now manager of Reading.

He wore the number seven shirt with distinction throughout the next two seasons as Reading finished third, then second, in Division Three (South) in the days when only one team was promoted. Although his best playing years were clearly behind him, he made thoughtful use of the ball and used tricks rather than speed to beat full-backs. His centres were accurate and he could still nip in to score the occasional goal.

Butler moved from the dressing room to the manger's office when he took over from Smith in 1935 and kept up Reading's challenge for promotion for the next four seasons. He made some astute signings, including several players with international experience, and also introduced more variety to the training regime. Tennis, basketball, netball, six-a-side tournaments and a new and fully equipped gymnasium and recreation room for the players all helped to break the monotony of lapping the track. He also intensified the club's youth policy and would not sign a player older than twenty-three unless he was of proven ability.

Butler took Reading close to promotion in each of his first three seasons in charge and also guided the club to success in the Division Three (South) Cup competition of 1937/38. He left abruptly in 1939 for personal reasons and took over at Guildford City.

During World War Two he became a PT instructor in the RAF, then later managed Torquay United before emigrating to South Africa. There he took charge of Johannesburg Rangers and later became a coach with the Rhodesian FA. He remained in South Africa until his death in 1966.

	First Team Appearances	Goals
Football League	169	0
FA Cup	17	0
FL Cup	8	0
Other	1	0
TOTAL	195	0

A Londoner by birth, Dennis Butler's first professional club was Chelsea, where he signed as a professional in 1960 after two years as a junior. At the time Chelsea were in the ascendancy and first team opportunities were limited, so he only played 18 League games for the Pensioners. He was transferred to Hull City for £10,000 in June 1963 and became the regular left-back in a solid defence which enabled the Yorkshire club to win the Third Division championship and reach round six of the FA Cup in 1965/66.

Butler kept his place in the Second Division team until 1969, when Jack Mansell brought the stocky, bow-legged defender to Elm Park as part of his rebuilding plans. The fee was again £10,000 and Butler proved to be just as good value for money as in his previous move.

He was difficult to dislodge from the team and, although his distribution may not have been particularly artistic, his effectiveness in the tackle was unmistakable. So strong and destructive were his interceptions that he became known to the Reading fans as 'Demolition Den'. His tackles were also invariably accompanied by a loud grunt – whether this was calculated to intimidate the opponent with the ball or increase the ferocity with which he made the challenge was never definitely established.

Suffice to say that he was one of the best full-backs in the lower divisions and that he captained the Reading side by proving himself to be a natural leader who set a consistently high standard. In his total of 418 Football League games, Dennis never scored a goal. The closest he came was in Reading's 1-1 draw away to Bristol Rovers on Boxing Day 1969, when, in his second game for the club, he was put clear with only the goalkeeper to beat. The home 'keeper hacked him down, Reading scored from the penalty and Butler was never to get as close to breaking his scoring duck again.

He was given a free transfer at the end of the 1973/74 season and concentrated on his painting and decorating business, which was based in Tilehurst. He also played part-time football for Margate in the Southern League. His son, Stephen, joined Reading as an apprentice but his career was curtailed by injury almost before it had begun.

Bobby Campbell
Utility player, 1954-1959

	First Team Appearances	Goals
Football League	94	12
FA Cup	15	1
FL Cup	0	0
Other	2	0
TOTAL	111	13

Bobby Campbell was well into the veteran stage of his career when he was brought to Elm Park by manager Jack Smith in the summer of 1954. He was a vastly experienced player, having made his debut for Falkirk aged nineteen in 1941. He lost some of his best footballing years to wartime soccer, but his talents were quickly recognised by the Scottish selectors when the game returned to normal, and he won 5 international caps for his country.

He joined Chelsea in May 1947 and was an immediate success, usually occupying the right-wing berth and becoming first choice in that position for the next six seasons. He made a total of 213 first team appearances for the London club, scoring 40 goals.

In his first season at Reading, Campbell occupied every forward position, as well as playing a few games at right half. He used his undoubted ability to read the game to save his legs and his best performances were reserved for Reading's FA Cup run, when the team were unlucky not to beat Manchester United in the 1-1 draw at Elm Park. Two seasons later he scored an outstanding individual goal in another cup match as Reading defeated Bedford Town from the Southern League 1-0.

As the years went by the regularity of his appearances declined, though he played in both full-back positions towards the end of his career with Reading. He spent two years at the club as coach from 1959 to 1961, then returned to Scotland to become manager of Dumbarton. The following year, in May 1962, he moved to Bristol Rovers as chief coach, a post he held until he was appointed manager in November 1977.

Campbell finally severed his connection with the West Country club after eighteen years when, in September 1980, he was appointed manager of Gloucester City. In 1982 he left Gloucester City and became a football coach with Bristol City Council.

Bryan Carnaby
Midfielder, 1972-1977

	First Team Appearances	Goals
Football League	145	10
FA Cup	9	0
FL Cup	15	0
Other	0	0
TOTAL	169	10

Geographically, Bryan Carnaby had as varied a career as any other Reading player. He played youth team football for Charlton Athletic and had trials with other League clubs before leaving for South Africa and playing there for two seasons.

When he returned to England he wrote to Reading for a trial, where he impressed manager Hurley. Carnaby made his first team debut against Crewe Alexandra on the opening day of the 1972/73 season. He scored after only eleven minutes in 1-1 draw.

He was the kind of player much admired by Charlie Hurley. Not overly skilful, but tough, wiry and competitive, he was a midfielder who would play his heart out for the full ninety minutes. As a result he became a regular in the team's midfield for the next five seasons as Reading struggled to win back their place in Division Three. They finally made it in 1975/76, and it was Carnaby who slid in to score the second goal in a 2-2 draw at Cambridge United on 21 April which ensured a return to the higher status.

Carnaby stayed for one more season, which unfortunately saw Reading relegated and the departure of the manager who rated him so highly. He went to play in Australia, returned to England to play non-League football for Carshalton and Wokingham, then became physiotherapist at Elm Park in the summer of 1980, taking over from Douggie Webb. He stayed in that post for only a year before the wanderlust overtook him again and he left for the United States to take up a coaching position in Atlanta, Georgia.

Bryan has returned to the Reading area on several occasions, mainly to look up old friends, but also to fit in a game of football or a training session whenever possible. Although he was never one of the stars in any of the teams in which he played, his reputation as a grafter and wholehearted battler remains undiminished

Darren Caskey

Midfield, 1995-present

	First Team Appearances	Goals
Football League	159	26
FA Cup	9	4
FL Cup	11	4
Other	5	1
TOTAL	**184**	**35**

Although the FA National School at Lilleshall closed in 1998, it had already educated (in football terms) a generation of young players whose influence is still significant in English soccer. A 1991 graduate of the establishment was Darren Caskey, who captained the England Under 18 team to victory in the 1993 UEFA Championships; his successful penalty kick enabled England to beat Turkey 1-0 in the final.

Caskey had joined Tottenham Hotspur as a schoolboy and, following his success with the England Youth team, made his Premiership debut for Spurs in January 1994. Although he made almost 50 first team appearances, he could never command a regular place. This was mainly due to the influx of foreign players at White Hart Lane so, after a loan spell with Watford, he decided to join Reading in April 1996.

The fee was £700,000, a record for Reading, but a gamble by joint managers Gooding and Quinn as they battled to keep the Royals in Division Two. Caskey gave an early sign of his prowess, as in the third minute of his first game, at home to Watford on 2 March 1996, he hit the bar with a superbly struck free kick from twenty-five yards. It was his first touch of the ball for his new club, and the closest either side came to scoring in a 0-0 draw.

Since that debut, Caskey has played under three more managers at Reading, but his performances have been characterised by two qualities. One is the ability to hit accurate, raking passes over forty or more yards distance and the other is his continuing marksmanship from dead ball situations. Any free kick awarded to Reading within striking range of the opposing goal will see him hit the target, using an effective combination of guile and power, and he is also the regular penalty taker. A shuffle in the run-up to the twelve-yard mark is sufficient to deceive most 'keepers and during the 1999/2000 season he scored 23 first team goals. This total established a new record for a Reading midfield player and also earned him selection for the PFA Division Two team. He was the only realistic choice as the fans' Player of the Season for that campaign.

Not surprisingly, his exploits have attracted attention from bigger clubs, but Caskey is still committed to Reading. It may be that his and the club's best years are yet to come.

Les Chappell

Forward, 1969-1975

	First Team Appearances	Goals
Football League	201	78
FA Cup	18	7
FL Cup	11	5
Other	1	0
TOTAL	231	90

A reliable goalscorer with lower division clubs, Les Chappell began his professional career with Rotherham United, where he played in the same side as Bobby Williams under the management of Jack Mansell. After three successful seasons he moved to Blackburn Rovers, but the goals did not come so frequently and he arrived at Reading on a free transfer in July 1969.

At Elm Park, Chappell linked up once more with Williams and Mansell and became one of the manager's small yet skilful forward line, which could seemingly score goals at will – while a porous defence was letting them in at the other end.

Chappell was the main threat up front because of his quickness in snapping up half-chances and he was a lethal finisher when given the ball in the penalty area. He finished as top scorer with 24 goals in his first season and his header in the 1-0 victory over Mansfield Town is still talked about as one of the most artistic ever seen at the ground.

He continued his exploits when Charlie Hurley replaced Mansell in the manager's office and in 1973/74 scored four League hat-tricks, including four goals against Torquay United, to equal Ron Blackman's record set in 1951/52. But for an injury

sustained in that match, he might well have ended the season as the Fourth Division's top scorer.

Chappell left Reading for Doncaster Rovers in December 1974 and stayed there for eighteen months before moving again, this time to Swansea City, where despite taking on a midfield role he continued to find the net.

He had scored 132 goals in 431 League appearances for his five clubs when he finished playing and became youth team manager, then first team coach at Swansea. He returned to Reading to live when he was appointed manager at Southern League Basingstoke Town, then more recently moved with his family to Torquay.

Alec Christie
Wing-half, 1919-1921

	First Team Appearances	Goals
Football League	31	1
FA Cup	1	0
FL Cup	0	0
Other	0	0
TOTAL	**32**	**1**

Born in Glasgow in 1896, Alec Christie began his football career with junior club Larkhill Thistle. He then joined Hamilton Academicals before enlisting in the Royal Navy, where he served as a decoder. He represented the Combined Services XI during the First World War, then on demobilisation signed for Reading. He made his debut in the Southern League against Exeter City, in the 1919/20 Victory Season, and became a regular member of the Reading side which played in the Football League Third Division in 1920/21.

He played at wing-half or inside forward, where his thoughtful passing set up frequent chances for other players. A tall, long-striding and popular team player, he could more than hold his own in the battles in midfield and it was a surprise when he left Reading at the end of the campaign. In his final game for the club he faced Southampton at Elm Park in the Royal Berkshire Hospital Charity Cup and, although the game was drawn 1-1, he received one of the winners' tankards on the toss of a coin.

Christie signed for Walsall in the summer of 1921, then subsequently played for Southampton, Norwich and Rochdale in the Football League. He ended his career at Aldershot, whom he assisted to win the Southern League title in 1930. He later returned to Reading to live and could recall, with great clarity even towards the end of his life, matches in which he had played over sixty years previously. He kept a house in Cressingham Road until his death at the age of eighty-four in 1981. His place in the history of the club is assured as one of the eleven who played in Reading's first Football League match.

He was one of the last survivors of that group and retained happy memories of his time at Elm Park. Although, as he explained in his declining years, the players had no choice other than to go full-time as Reading entered the Football League, it was an experience he never regretted.

Syd Crawford

Goalkeeper, 1913-1922

	First Team Appearances	Goals
Football League	73	0
FA Cup	5	0
FL Cup	0	0
Other	0	0
TOTAL	78	0

Born in Dundee in 1887, H.S. 'Syd' Crawford began as a goalkeeper with Newcastle United, but did not make their first team before moving to join Arsenal. He had more luck and found better form with the Gunners and played 27 Football League First Division games for them between 1911 and 1913.

He arrived at Reading in the summer of 1913 and combined playing for Reading in Division One of the Southern League with his weekday trade as a bookbinder at Cox & Wymans. Then the First World War intervened; Crawford volunteered for active service and fought in France with the Army Service Corps, though he still managed to fit in the occasional game of football with his unit.

When peace returned he came back to Elm Park and played for one more season in the Southern League before Reading became founder members of the Football League's Third Division in 1920. He kept goal in the club's first ever Football League match, a 1-0 victory away to Newport County, on Saturday 28 August 1920. He had much to do with Reading's victory, as the *South Wales Argus* described him as 'playing the game of his life', and only he stood between the home team and a deserved equaliser.

Crawford missed only two of Reading's League games that season, but his best displays were reserved for the three epic FA Cup ties against Chelsea. He was an outstanding penalty-kick saver, and in the first tie had to face a penalty kick in the last seconds of the game. He made a prodigious leap to deflect the kick to one side – so great was the excitement that Crawford's wife, plus Canon Gilmour, a club director, who were sitting in the packed Elm Park stand, both fainted.

Crawford saved five penalty kicks in a row that season and gained national recognition for his peculiar way of dealing with them. He had the technique of standing near one post – on the assumption that he would only then have one direction in which to dive – which seemed to unnerve a succession of opponents.

He stayed with Reading until the end of the 1921/22 campaign then was transferred to Millwall for £50. He spent three seasons with that club, then moved back to the North to live in Whitley Bay.

Gordon Cumming
Forward, 1969-1978

	First Team Appearances	Goals
Football League	295	51
FA Cup	22	8
FL Cup	14	2
Other	1	1
TOTAL	332	62

Gordon Cumming was born in Johnstone and started his career with Inverness Caledonians before moving south to join Arsenal. He won Scottish youth international caps whilst with the London club, but only progressed as far as their reserve team. He was signed for Reading by manager Jack Mansell in December 1969 for £8,000, as a replacement for Tom Jenkins, and went straight into the first team. He scored in his first League match, a 3-1 win over Stockport County on 13 December 1969, and quickly replaced Jenkins in the crowd's affections.

Cumming was the kind of neat, tricky forward much admired by the manager and he could score goals too, being top scorer in 1970/71 and 1971/72. In the latter season he was elected Player of the Season by a huge majority. When Charlie Hurley took over from Mansell as manager, he began to play Cumming in a deeper role in midfield, but the Scot continued to flourish and was captain of the side which won promotion from Division Four in the 1975/76 season.

Two games in which he played remain particularly in the memory. One was the 8-0 thrashing of Southport in April 1970, when Cumming completed his only hat-trick for the club, and the other was the 1-2 defeat by Arsenal in the FA Cup in February 1972, when he was generally agreed to be the best player in the Reading side against his former team.

Cumming left Elm Park in the summer of 1978. He joined the family catering business but carried on playing football for local club Highmoor in the Reading Combination League, where he also took on coaching duties.

When Reading were drawn to play Manchester United in the FA Cup, in 1996, Cumming was interviewed by the BBC. Not only was he asked to forecast the result, but the BBC also broadcast film of him scoring against Manchester United in the Watney Cup game played twenty-six seasons previously.

Hugh Davey

Forward, 1924-1928

	First Team Appearances	Goals
Football League	56	46
FA Cup	5	3
FL Cup	0	0
Other	0	0
TOTAL	61	49

A native of Belfast, where he was born on the first day of 1899, Hugh Davey played for Glentoran in the Irish League before joining Blackburn Rovers on loan. He failed to make a first team appearance for the Lancashire club but persisted in trying to make the breakthrough into English football and eventually signed for Bournemouth while they were still in the Southern League.

In January 1925 he was part of a player-exchange deal which took Reading full-back Rob Marshall to Bournemouth and saw Davey come to Elm Park. He struggled to make the first team to start with. However, a hat-trick on the last day of the 1924/25 season in a 4-1 win over Bristol Rovers confirmed his place at centre forward for the following campaign.

He played only 24 League games during the Third Division (South) championship of 1925/26, mainly due to a series of injuries, but also because he was by now being selected for the Northern Ireland international team. Even so, he was leading scorer that season, with 23 goals, including another hat-trick on the final day when Reading beat Brentford 7-1 to secure the title.

Davey made intermittent appearances for the first team in Division Two and scored the club's first goal at the new level in a 1-3 defeat at Blackpool. He was absent for most of the FA Cup run, but was recalled to the forward line in place of Teddy Braithwaite for the semi-final against Cardiff City, when Reading were knocked out of the competition.

Despite being on the short side, Davey was a brave, aggressive leader of the line, shooting cleverly with both feet and unafraid to join in the fiercest of goalmouth melees. He made a total of four appearances for his country while with Reading, scoring against England, and won one further cap with Portsmouth, whom he joined in December 1927. After only 8 first team games for the South Coast club he left on a free transfer in May 1928.

Bill Davies

Centre half, 1954-1961

W. DAVIES *(Reading)*

	First Team Appearances	Goals
Football League	202	0
FA Cup	15	0
FL Cup	1	0
Other	8	0
TOTAL	226	0

Bill Davies was the archetypal Third Division centre half. He was not especially quick, skilful or pretty to watch, but for seven seasons he performed solidly and reliably at the heart of Reading's defence. He rarely ventured over the halfway line, and any ball that came near him in the penalty area usually ended up being belted into touch or headed back whence it came. He accepted all the knocks that came his way, accumulating countless cuts and bruises, but never flinched in the service of his team.

He had been brought up in a tough school – he was a junior at Hull City and then Leeds United without making a first team appearance – and signed for Reading in January 1953 while on National Service. Apart from one game at right-half and another at centre forward, both in his first season at Elm Park, he played every of his games for the club wearing the number five

shirt.

He lost his place for a while to the emerging talent of the young Dick Spiers, but recovered to play in every game of the 1958/59 campaign, and his consistency was recognised by selection for the Football Combination XI which played a Dutch XI in Amsterdam in April 1959. He had also been a member of the Third Division (South) team which met their Northern counterparts a season earlier.

Steady but not spectacular, Davies completed well over 200 brave, battling displays in a Reading shirt. He never scored a first team goal, as his moves upfield were limited to the occasional foray when he had time to try and get his head to a corner kick.

He left Reading in 1961 and combined playing for Southern League Dover with running his own engineering business. He did return to Reading briefly in 1971/72 to help his old friend, Jimmy Wallbanks, when the latter took over from Jack Mansell as caretaker-manager. He is a regular in attendance at football reunions held in the town.

Steve Death

Goalkeeper, 1969-1982

	First Team Appearances	Goals
Football League	471	0
FA Cup	33	0
FL Cup	32	0
Other	1	0
TOTAL	537	0

Reading's greatest goalkeeper of all time, Steve Death, continued a tradition of small yet fearless custodians at Elm Park. Born in 1949, he was preferred to Peter Shilton in the England Schools international team and joined West Ham United from school. He had all the technical attributes of a First Division goalkeeper, but being just 5 feet 7 inches tall he was the shortest goalkeeper in the League. He was restricted to just one first team game with the Hammers, against Manchester City in 1969.

He joined Reading on loan that same year, making his debut and keeping a clean sheet in a 1-0 win against Brighton on 6 November 1969. He remained first choice for the rest of the season, and was voted Player of the Season by the fans. Death signed for Reading in August 1970 for £20,000, at the time a club record, and made the goalkeeping position his own for the next decade.

He made up for his lack of height with amazing agility, bravery and sound judgement. He excelled in one-on-one situations, became an expert penalty kick saver and some of his stops verged on the miraculous. He shared in all Reading's triumphs and disasters during the 1970s, being a regular in the promotion teams of 1976 and 1979 and also the one which was relegated in 1977.

Death picked up several awards, winning a Division Four championship medal in 1978/79, PFA Divisional Awards for Division Four in 1973/74 and 1978/79, and more Player of the Season trophies for 1972/73, 1973/74 and 1976/77. In addition, he set a Reading club record for 156 consecutive first team appearances between August 1978 and April 1981. At one stage he also held the record for the number of appearances in the major competitions of Football League, FA Cup and Football League Cup, until surpassed by Martin Hicks.

His Football League record, which still stands, is that of keeping eleven consecutive clean sheets at the end of the 1978/79 Championship season, during which he played in every game. He did not concede a

Steve Death punches the ball away from the Exeter City attack. Reading won this game 2-1 on 20 October 1979.

goal for 1,103 minutes and, when he was eventually beaten, it was by an own goal from one of his full-backs.

Although a quiet and shy person, he was incredibly popular with the fans and Death enjoyed a well-deserved testimonial in November 1979. He lost his place in the first team in 1981 and finally left Elm Park in the summer of 1982. He returned to his native Suffolk and played for his village side in Elmswell for a handful of games. More recently he has made his home back in Reading and is working as a greenkeeper at Mapledurham golf course.

Although he is often seen in and around Reading, Death's reserved nature means that he does not attend players' reunions or give interviews when asked to do so. This should not be seen as a sign of aloofness, however, rather the opposite. He was always too modest to talk about his own ability, although he could hold an articulate conversation about the techniques and tactics of goalkeeping.

Kerry Dixon
Striker, 1980-1983

	First Team Appearances	Goals
Football League	116	51
FA Cup	3	0
FL Cup	6	0
Other	7	6
TOTAL	132	57

The ability of Maurice Evans to introduce promising youngsters from non-League football into the Football League was never better illustrated than in the case of Kerry Dixon. Dixon played youth team football for Spurs, was released, signed for Dunstable and became the Southern League's top scorer with 52 goals in 1979/80.

Evans signed him for £25,000 in the 1980 close season and, although still a part-timer, he top-scored for Reading with 13 League goals. He scored one fewer in 1981/82, but the season after that was the top scorer in Division Three with 26 goals from just 35 matches. That feat was remarkable for the fact that it was achieved with a relegated team.

Dixon's prowess was recognised by his selection for the PFA Division Three side. Dixon was quick, brave, had a lethal shot in both feet and his close control was good too. His ability was noticed by bigger clubs, and in August 1983 he joined Chelsea for a Reading club record of £150,000.

He repeated his scoring exploits with the London club and his 28 goals in his first season with them helped his new team gain promotion to Division One. He completed an extraordinary hat-trick by becoming Division One's leading scorer with 36 goals

in 1984/85 and England selection soon followed. He represented his country 8 times in full internationals, earning Reading a further £25,000 by so doing.

Dixon remained with Chelsea until 1992, totalling 147 goals in 335 League games. He then played for Southampton, Millwall and Luton Town before a brief spell as player-manager of Doncaster Rovers. After that experience he dropped down into non-League football once again and combined running a pub with appearing, still as a striker, with Boreham Wood of the Rymans Isthmian League.

During the 2000/2001 season, Kerry is manager of Letchworth, who play in the Minerva Spartan League. Dixon transformed the club's fortunes in the year 2000.

Mike Dixon
Goalkeeper, 1962-1968

	First Team Appearances	Goals
Football League	113	0
FA Cup	9	0
FL Cup	12	0
Other	0	0
TOTAL	134	0

Mike Dixon attended Caversham Secondary School and was an outstanding young goalkeeper who represented England Schoolboys against Ireland and Germany in 1959. He signed for Reading, his home town club, in the same year and worked his way through the youth and reserve teams before making his first team debut at Notts County on 6 September 1962. For the next three seasons he understudied Arthur Wilkie, but made the position his own in 1965/66.

His attributes as a fearless, acrobatic last line of defence were appreciated by the supporters, who elected him as Player of the Season for 1967/68, even though he was a part-timer. He trained with the amateur players on midweek evenings, combining his football with managing a newsagent's shop in Tilehurst.

One of his greatest displays for the club came in a 0-0 draw away to Manchester City in a 1968 FA Cup game, though he was beaten seven times in the replay. Dixon was always very good at dealing with spot kicks and saved more than his fair share of penalties. He left Reading in the summer of 1969 and continued his part-time career at Aldershot, where he made 38 League appearances.

A true lover of football, Dixon qualified as a referee and took charge of games in local parks when not selected for professional duties. He became secretary of Wokingham Town in the Isthmian League, and extended his goalkeeping career with that club for several more seasons.

Mike Dixon was always keen to encourage schools and youth football and put so much back into the game he loved. It was a great tragedy that he should die at the early age of forty-nine in 1993.

Mike's two sons, Kevin and Paul, both became postmen and were also noted local footballers. Paul showed particular promise and made a number of appearances for Reading Reserves during the late 1980s, although he never reached first team level.

Tommy Dixon

Centre forward, 1954-1959

	First Team Appearances	Goals
Football League	123	63
FA Cup	10	6
FL Cup	0	0
Other	10	7
TOTAL	143	76

A true 'Geordie', Tommy Dixon was born in Newcastle and played his early football as a member of the local Boys' Brigade team at left-back. He moved to centre forward in Army games during his National Service and signed for Newcastle United as an amateur after leaving the Forces.

He joined West Ham United as a professional in 1952 and immediately made an impression as a goalscorer. In 1953/54 he headed the Hammers scoring list with 19 goals, but surprisingly only played in 4 League games the following season. He was considered a good catch when he came to Reading in March 1955 and became the seventh centre forward the club had tried that season. He was injured on his debut but soon recaptured his goalscoring ability and was the Biscuitmen's leading scorer in both 1956/57 and 1957/58.

Some of his early appearances for Reading were as a left-winger, but he looked far more comfortable when leading the line. Although he favoured his left foot, he could find the back of the net equally well with his right and was a strong header of the ball. Curiously, the vast majority of his shots and headers either went over the bar or in the net – they were very rarely wide or at the goalkeeper. His style of marksmanship was so pronounced that he was known to the fans behind the goal as 'Over the bar' Dixon.

His scoring ratio at Reading was a good one, however, and on three occasions he scored four times in a League match. Dixon was quick, and once he had got into his stride his long legs could help him outpace any defender as he ran on to through passes and crosses.

He lost his place to Bobby Ayre during the 1958/59 campaign and moved to Brighton & Hove Albion, where he remained for a couple of seasons before moving back to his native North-East. He ended his playing days with a couple of seasons with Wokington then two more with Barrow. The goals continued to flow as they had done throughout his professional career and by the time he retired he had accumulated the respectable total of 136 goals scored in 312 League matches.

43

Joe Duckworth

Goalkeeper, 1924-1930

	First Team Appearances	Goals
Football League	202	0
FA Cup	23	0
FL Cup	0	0
Other	0	0
TOTAL	225	0

The arrival of goalkeeper Joe Duckworth from Aberdare Athletic coincided with Reading's successful period in the late 1920s. He was small but fearless and began a tradition of safe keeping which was to be carried on by many of his successors between the posts.

Duckworth made his debut at the beginning of the 1924/25 season and was such a model of consistency that he missed only one first team game over the next four years. He played in every match in the Division Three (South) Championship campaign of 1925/26 and was also ever-present during the epic ten match FA Cup run of 1926/27 when Reading reached the semi-final stage.

His greatest display for Reading almost certainly came in the 1-0 FA Cup victory over Sheffield Wednesday in January 1929. Wednesday were to become First Division champions that season, but Reading, and especially Duckworth, were too good for them at Elm Park.

John Arlott described the diminutive goalkeeper's part in the win thus: 'I was behind the Reading goal that afternoon in the second half and the ball seemed perpetually before my face. Why Wednesday did not score only heaven and Joe Duckworth could tell you – and I suspect Duckworth would not be too certain. Once Allen broke through and Duckworth dived forwards a full nine feet to push the ball off his shooting foot. It flew to Hooper, and Duckworth, halfway up from his knees, pushed the winger's shot in the air, caught it as Allen charged him, then mis-kicked it clear to Seed, whose header he turned over the bar.'

So this was Duckworth's life in the Reading goal – hectic, sometimes confused, often muddy and dangerous, but never dull. He served the club well for over 200 games before leaving Reading in 1930 for two seasons with Brighton & Hove Albion and one with York City.

In later life he worked as a deckchair attendant on Blackpool beach and in 1992 his Third Division (South) Championship medal was found in a car boot sale in Manchester.

Pat Earles
Forward, 1976-1983

	First Team Appearances	Goals
Football League	247	68
FA Cup	9	6
FL Cup	22	11
Other	6	0
TOTAL	**284**	**85**

Pat Earles was an England schoolboy international in 1970, the same year that he joined Southampton, his local club, as an apprentice. He was upgraded to full professional status in 1973, but first team opportunities were limited. He did make the Saints' FA Cup winning squad of 1976, but failed to gain even a place on the bench at Wembley.

After just 14 first team games he was signed by manager Charlie Hurley for Reading in January 1977, at a cost of £15,000. He was bought to stop Hurley's team from sliding into Division Four and although he was unable to do that, he did give evidence of the goals that his pace and knowledge of the game might bring in a stronger team.

Earles flourished once Maurice Evans had replaced Hurley as manager. He was the club's second highest scorer in 1977/78, his 15 League goals leaving him one behind Ollie Kearns, but the following season, 1978/79, he top-scored with 15 again as Reading became champions of Division Four.

A cool and composed finisher, he continued to rattle in the goals over the next four seasons. Few of them were headers, but he had the ability to strike the ball extremely hard with either foot and this, together with the superb timing of his runs between defenders, meant that he was always threatening to score. He was very rarely dropped from the side and it was only as his speed began to diminish that the goals began to dry up.

His last year with Reading was the relegation campaign of 1982/83. One of the most intelligent footballers to represent the club, he was given a free transfer and joined RS Southampton, where he combined part-time football with a new career as a probation officer.

When RS Southampton folded, Earles moved back to Bognor Regis town and made a number of appearances in that club's Isthmian League team. Even in his non-League days, he maintained his reputation as a clean, sporting competitor.

Maurice Edelston

Inside forward, 1939-1952

	First Team Appearances	Goals
Football League	202	70
FA Cup	21	10
FL Cup	0	0
Other	0	0
TOTAL	**223**	**80**

Any selection of an all-time Reading XI would be certain to include Maurice Edelston, not only at inside forward but also as captain, as he was one of the most inspirational skippers the club has ever had.

He had the perfect footballing background. His father had been a professional with Manchester City, Fulham, Nelson and Hull City and arrived at Elm Park in 1939 as manager. Maurice, who had represented Great Britain in the 1936 Berlin Olympic Games and already played for Brentford and Fulham as an amateur, came with him. He played in the aborted 1939/40 season for Reading, but was called up into the Army.

Whilst in the forces he was a regular in the England team and also played numerous representative matches for the Army and Combined Services. He helped Reading win the London War Cup against Brentford in 1941 and after the cessation of hostilities returned to Elm Park to claim a regular place in the team.

Still an amateur, he scored a hat-trick in Reading's record 10-2 victory over Crystal Palace on 4 September 1946 and three more in the 7-2 win against Southend United three days later. He is still the only amateur to score hat-tricks in consecutive games. He was acting as club secretary that season due to his father's illness, but was upgraded to full professional status when Ted Drake was appointed manager in June 1947.

Maurice, a London University graduate, had also been teaching at the Bluecoat School in Sonning, but now turned his full attention to getting Reading into Division Two. Reading were runners-up in 1948/49 and 1951/52, when only one team was promoted from the Third Division (South), and Edelston was the mainspring behind those near misses. He was a cogent, perceptive passer of the ball who could create and also take scoring chances, as well as being a natural leader of his team. He reached double figures in each of his six seasons with Reading, yet also found time to open a sports shop in partnership with Gordon Brice.

Maurice left Reading for Northampton Town in 1952 and later became one of the BBC's leading sports commentators. He led a full and varied life and it was a tragedy when he died in 1977, at the age of fifty-seven, following a heart attack whilst working at the BBC.

Maurice Edelston scores during the 10-2 victory over Crystal Palace.

Skipper Edelston discusses the location of a Reading free-kick with the referee.

Bert Eggo

Right back, 1921-1929

ROBERT M. EGGO

	First Team Appearances	Goals
Football League	289	2
FA Cup	23	0
FL Cup	0	0
Other	0	0
TOTAL	312	2

Born in Brechin in 1895, Bert Eggo's first professional club was Heart of Midlothian, but he came south of the border in 1919 to join Sheffield Wednesday. He stayed with that club for two seasons, making 23 first team appearances, all at right half, without scoring.

He lost his place in the Wednesday team through pleurisy, and travelled further south to join Reading on a free transfer in the 1921 close season. He remained in the half-back line for his first two seasons at Elm Park, but was converted to right-back in October 1923 and missed only five games in that position in the following five seasons. He was a model of consistency and appointed as club captain for one of the most successful periods in Reading's history.

Eggo was outstanding in the Division Three (South) championship team of 1925/26 and also during the following season's FA Cup run, which took Reading to the semi-finals. Not especially tall, he had the knack of timing his tackles to perfection and inspired his colleagues with his doughty but scrupulously fair play.

He made more first team appearances (312 in total) for Reading than any other pre-Second World War player and was rewarded with a testimonial game against Tottenham Hotspur in 1928, the same year that he retired from playing. He then returned to Scotland and, in 1951, when the Reading team travelled to Dundee to play a Festival of Britain friendly match, one of the first people to greet them was Eggo, now working on the staff of a Dundee hospital. One of the heroes of Elm Park's golden era, Bert Eggo died in 1977.

It should be noted that Eggo is in the top fifteen appearance-makers for the club. Bearing in mind that far fewer games were played in the pre-World War Two seasons, his achievement is all the more remarkable. In those days, however, agents were unheard of and players were far more loyal to their clubs.

	First Team Appearances	Goals
Football League	122	11
FA Cup	19	0
FL Cup	0	0
Other	0	0
TOTAL	141	11

Born at Abercanaid near Merthyr in 1902, David Evans was a stylish, constructive wing-half who had played for Merthyr Tydfil, Nelson and Bolton Wanderers before joining Reading in August 1924. He arrived in exchange for Harry Cockerill and quickly settled into the first team at left half alongside the reliable Alf Messer. He could play neat, constructive football and was a terrier in the tackle, but was not entirely consistent and this led to his absence from the side on occasions.

Evans was at his best during the Third Division championship season of 1925/26, when he also played for a brief period at centre forward after Davey had been injured. He was immensely popular with the crowd and had the habit of stopping to chat with supporters just before he took the field. An expert penalty-kick taker, he had a high ratio of successes from the spot, always approaching the task coolly.

He stayed in the first team for two more seasons, playing in every match of the 1926/27 FA Cup run, which took Reading to the semi-finals. He won 4 Welsh international caps whilst at Elm Park and when he was transferred to Huddersfield in June 1928, the fee of £6,200 was a record for both clubs. He was part of a large squad at Huddersfield, however, and never established himself in the first team.

He subsequently moved on to Bury, then to Merthyr again and finally to Burton Town, where he spent the 1932/33 season as player-manager before retiring from football.

Thereafter he worked at Hoovers of Merthyr, taking little interest in football. He pawned his caps and medals when times were hard and died of cancer at the age of forty-nine in 1951.

In recent times his descendants have contacted Reading Football Club, in an attempt to find more details about his time at Elm Park. They were told that mere statistics do scant justice to a vastly entertaining player who excited crowds wherever he went.

Maurice Evans
Wing-half, 1955-1967

	First Team Appearances	Goals
Football League	407	13
FA Cup	26	3
FL Cup	15	0
Other	11	0
TOTAL	**459**	**16**

It is doubtful whether any of the players to appear in Reading's first team has had a greater affection for or influence on the club than Maurice Evans. He began his football career with Didcot Athletic Minors, was selected for the English Boys Clubs team which played the German Boys Clubs and signed for Reading as a ground staff junior at the age of sixteen in 1952.

He soon won his place at left-half in the first team and held it throughout the adversities of National Service in the RAF. On his return to civilian life, he made the wing-half position his own for the next ten seasons, with an occasional appearance at inside-left or, later in his career, at full-back. A skilful, thoughtful player without an ounce of malice in him, he was respected by team-mates, opponents and spectators in equal measure for his sportsmanship and dedication to the game. He was never booked in 459 first team games, a total

exceeded only by Martin Hicks, Steve Death and Dick Spiers. He might well have moved to a bigger club, but decided to remain loyal to his only professional team. Rewards for his dedication were scant: selection for the Football Combination XI versus a Dutch XI in 1958, a place as non-playing reserve for the Third Division (South) against the Third (North) in the same season and two Southern Floodlit Cup runners-up medals.

But he was not concerned about rewards. It was enough to play for the club he loved and a matter of great sadness when he was released in 1967. He took over as player-manager at Andover for a brief period before joining Shrewsbury Town as trainer-coach and becoming their manager in 1972. He returned to Elm Park as assistant manager to Charlie Hurley in 1974, and when the latter was sacked three years later became caretaker manager.

He managed the 1978/79 team which won the Division Four championship. His style was that of careful, thoughtful organisation, added to a depth of personality which inspired and encouraged those around him. He was a highly proficient coach too and was deservedly named Fourth Division Manager of the Season. He remained manager at Elm Park

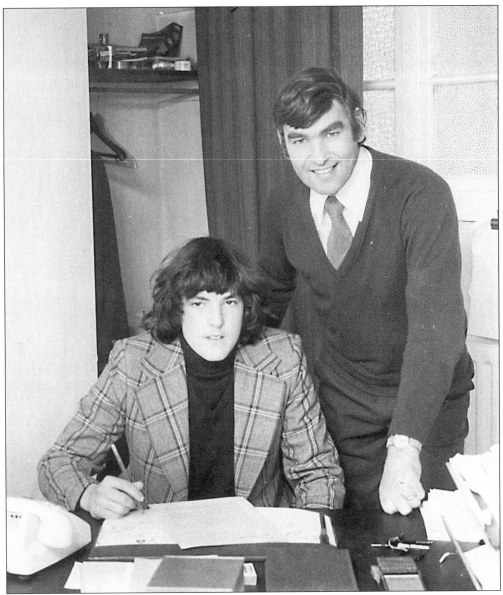

In his role as Reading manager, Maurice Evans signs a young Jerry Williams in 1976.

for seven years, making perceptive signings from non-League football such as Kerry Dixon and Trevor Senior, but was sacked rather surprisingly in January 1984. He moved on to Oxford United as coach and was their manager when they won the Milk Cup in 1986 and also reached Division One for the first time.

He was later appointed to the Oxford board of directors, but returned to his spiritual home in 1999 when he came back to Reading Football Club as chief scout. He died suddenly on 18 August 2000, having attended the training ground earlier in the day.

Alan Foster
Inside left, 1911-1915

	First Team Appearances	Goals
Football League	0	0
FA Cup	13	3
FL Cup	0	0
Other	0	0
TOTAL	**13**	**3**

Alan Foster spent two seasons with Bristol City from 1909 to 1911 whilst the club were in the Football League's First Division, but spent most of that time playing for City's reserve team. He did manage a total of 13 first team games, scoring once, before being transferred to Reading, who had been impressed by his displays for City Reserves against Reading Reserves in a Great Western Suburban League match.

The fee was £75, paid in two instalments as Reading were struggling financially, but never was money better spent. Reading had won the Southern League Division Two the previous season and achieved mid-table respectability in Division One in 1911/12. Foster was the genius in the team. A consummate strategist, he could spray passes around him with pinpoint accuracy – no easy task when the ball was as heavy as lead and the pitches resembled a ploughed field for much of the fixture list. He had great leadership skills too, captaining the team on many occasions, and his most memorable display in a Reading shirt came when Reading faced First Division Aston Villa, who included nine internationals in their line-up, in the second round of the FA Cup. The first game at Villa Park was drawn 1-1, and for the replay at Elm Park, Reading's directors increased the admission price to three shillings for the grandstand. Nobody objected, however, as Reading defeated their illustrious opponents 1-0, with Foster scoring the only goal of the game at precisely 3.20 p.m., after Fred Bartholemew had 'diddled' a defender. The Villa club were so enraptured by Foster's performance that they attempted to buy him immediately after the game. Their bid was £650, a massive fee at the time, but such was the outcry from the Reading supporters that the board were forced to decline the offer.

Reading enjoyed excellent FA Cup runs and improved placings in the Southern League during the rest of Foster's time at Elm Park. The inside left was an ever-present in the 1914/15 season, when the team finished as runners-up to Watford and the inside forward trio of Jimmy Chorley, Joe Bailey and Foster totalled 45 goals between them. At the end of that season, however, the FA suspended all League and cup football and many players, Foster among them, went overseas to fight for their country against Germany. Tragically, Foster was killed in action on 8 August 1916, his death robbing Reading of one of its greatest players.

Steve Francis

Goalkeeper, 1986-1993

	First Team Appearances	Goals
Football League	216	0
FA Cup	15	0
FL Cup	15	0
Other	13	0
TOTAL	259	0

When Ian Branfoot signed goalkeeper Steve Francis from Chelsea for £20,000 in February 1986, he described his acquisition as a 'snip'; he was proved correct many times over.

Francis was only twenty-two when he joined Reading, but he already had considerable experience with the London club, whom he had represented for seven seasons. He had been the regular first-team 'keeper for two full seasons and earned a Full Members' Cup winners medal in 1986. He lost his place to Eddie Niedzwiecki, however, and came to Elm Park.

He went straight into the side and held his place, apart from absence due to injury, for the next six seasons. Although not especially tall or big for a 'keeper, he more than made up for those shortcomings with his exquisitely safe handling of the ball, plus excellent anticipation. His reflexes were quick too and these qualities made him one of the most respected goalkeepers in the lower divisions.

The high point of his career at Reading came during the incredible Simod Cup run of 1987/88, when he saved two penalties in the semi-final shootout against Coventry City, then played superbly in the 4-1 win against Luton Town at Wembley in the final.

He lost his place to a succession of loan goalkeepers in 1991/92, then to his eventual replacement, Shaka Hislop, the following season. Even when he left Elm Park in the summer of 1993, Reading made a more than healthy profit on their original deal by selling him to Huddersfield Town for a fee of £150,000, decided by a Football League tribunal.

He remained a steady last line of defence with the Yorkshire club, adding more than 200 first team appearances to his career record over the next six seasons.

In January 1999, he was allowed to join Northampton Town on a free transfer, where he made his debut against Reading. He bowed out of the Football League at the end of the 1998/99 season.

Robin Friday

Forward, 1973-1977

	First Team Appearances	Goals
Football League	121	46
FA Cup	3	2
FL Cup	11	5
Other	0	0
TOTAL	135	53

One of the most charismatic players ever to wear a Reading shirt, Robin Friday had a relatively brief yet spectacular Football League career. He had trials with Reading as a youngster, but was rejected and drifted into non-League football whilst working on building sites. He was spotted by manager Charlie Hurley when he played twice for Hayes against Reading in the FA Cup in 1972 and arrived on trial at Elm Park the following year.

Robin made an impression right from the start. In his first training session with the club he went around clattering experienced professionals until Hurley told him to stop. He made his debut away to Northampton Town on 27 January 1974 and created two of Reading's goals in a 3-3 draw. On his home debut he scored twice in a 4-1 win over Exeter City and quickly endeared himself to the fans with his outrageously cheeky style of play. He scored against Doncaster with an incredible swerving low drive and his turn and volley to find the net against Tranmere Rovers in March 1976 brought applause even from the referee, and is reckoned as one of the best goals ever seen at Elm Park.

He was the supporters' Player of the Season for 1974/75 and 1975/76 and contributed greatly to the promotion to Division Three, which was achieved in the latter season. He would also have been elected to the PFA Divisional team on more than one occasion but for the fact that he was not a member of the union.

It could not last, of course, because Friday was so temperamental and unpredictable. Hurley had handled him as well as any manager could, but Friday was sold to Cardiff City in December 1976 for £30,000. He had played 135 first team games for Reading, scored 53 goals, been cautioned twenty times but sent off only once. He had captured the imagination of the fans, young and old, as few other players have done and his individuality was typified by an incident in a home game against Rochdale. He scored a last-minute winner in a 2-1 victory, then promptly ran off the pitch and kissed a policeman!

In his first game for Cardiff City he scored twice, despite being marked by

Robin's spectacular style made him the idol of many young fans.

Bobby Moore, now with Fulham. He played only 21 League games for the Welsh club, scoring 6 times, before leaving to return to London and find work as an asphalter and decorator. He trained for a while with Brentford, but by now his health was deteriorating and he died aged only thirty-eight in 1990.

But his memory lives on. He had a book entitled *The Greatest Footballer You Never Saw* written about him in 1997 and in 1999, he was voted by Reading supporters as the club's Player of the Century. The award was collected by his daughter, Arabella. Although some older, more traditional supporters were surprised, even disappointed when Friday was given this accolade because of his poor behaviour on the field, it was a true reflection of the impression he left on the club. No player, before or since, will be remembered for such extremes of behaviour and eccentricity.

Michael Gilkes

Left-wing, 1984-1998

	First Team Appearances	Goals
Football League	393	43
FA Cup	34	1
FL Cup	32	6
Other	28	2
TOTAL	487	52

Michael Gilkes must have thought his chance of a career in professional football had vanished when Leicester City released him as a nineteen year old in 1984. However, the Reading manager of the time, Maurice Evans, made yet another of his intuitive signings and brought Gilkes to Elm Park, where he immediately made his mark as a lightning-quick left-winger in the Football Combination.

Michael's first team debut came as a substitute against Lincoln City on 27 October 1984/ and although that game was lost 1-5, he recovered from the disappointment to gain an almost permanent place in the starting line-up. He won a Third Division Championship medal in 1985/86 as Ian Branfoot's team raced away with the title and became feared among Division Two defenders as one of the slickest and quickest wide players in the game. He was at his best when given a pass from midfield to run on to, so that he could outpace or trick his opposing full-back, sprint to the by-line, then cross with precision for the strikers to fire at goal.

He is probably best remembered for his part in the 1987/88 season when, although Reading were relegated, the team enjoyed that marvellous run in the Simod Cup competition. Five First Division teams were beaten that season, Michael converting the penalty kick in the semi-final shootout against Coventry City which took the Royals to Wembley and scoring Reading's first goal in the 4-1 triumph over Luton Town in the final. He gave his greatest performance in a Reading shirt on that afternoon of Sunday 27 March 1988.

He continued to play for Reading for another ten seasons, often as the mercurial winger who was the idol of the South Bank, sometimes as a penetrating left-back (as wing-backs suddenly became fashionable). He won a Division Two Championship medal under Mark McGhee in 1993/94 and was selected for the Football League XI versus the Army FA in 1988. Only six players have made more League appearances for Reading and he was given a well-deserved testimonial game at Elm Park in July 1998.

He was transferred from Reading to Wolverhampton Wanderers the same year, having had loan spells at Chelsea and

Michael Gilkes scores a late winner in a 1-0 victory over Bristol City on 14 December1985.

Southampton earlier in his career. Injury restricted his opportunities with Wolves, but he spent the 1999/2000 season with Millwall, where his pace even now continues to stimulate supporters and bamboozle defenders. In 2000 he finally earned international recognition by representing Barbados in World Cup qualifying games.

Playing for his country was a fitting finale to a long and outstanding football career which nearly ended before it had begun. He had won a variety of honours, including third place in a professional footballers' sprint championship, and amassed a total of almost six hundred first class games. Elm Park crowds will remember him not just for the fact that he played the game with a smile on his face, but because he was the quickest player they had ever seen in a Reading shirt.

Gilbert Glidden

Inside left, 1936-1950

	First Team Appearances	Goals
Football League	111	24
FA Cup	8	1
FL Cup	0	0
Other	3	1
TOTAL	122	26

One of only four players to make pre- and post-Second World War appearances in the Football League for Reading, Gilbert Glidden was an England schoolboy international in 1930. He represented his country against Wales, and joined his local club, Sunderland, on leaving school. He failed to make their first team and moved to Port Vale in 1935. There he stayed for only one season, scoring a single goal in 5 League appearances, before journeying south to Elm Park.

He struggled to make an impression in the seasons leading up to the war, but did gain a Division Three (Southern Section) Cup winners medal in 1938. He played in both legs of the final, when Reading beat Bristol City 6-2 on aggregate. He had played in every forward position as well as at half-back whilst trying to establish himself in the side.

After the end of hostilities he found a more permanent berth at inside left. Maurice Edelston was the other inside forward and the two of them were as perceptive a pair of passers of the ball as a Third Division team could wish for.

But the war years had taken a large chunk out of Glidden's career and he never realised his full potential. Despite this, he was a loyal servant to Reading FC and his time with the club spanned fourteen seasons. He was a fitness fanatic and ran a 'keep fit' club at 68 London Street. He was interested in coaching too, and became the coach of local team Tilehurst City, who played in the Reading Institute League.

Glidden left Reading in 1950 and transferred to Leyton Orient, making just one League appearance for them in the penultimate game of the 1950/51 season. He died, aged 73, in 1988.

Mick Gooding
Midfielder, 1989-1997

	First Team Appearances	Goals
Football League	314	26
FA Cup	19	2
FL Cup	19	0
Other	16	2
TOTAL	368	30

Mick Gooding was already a vastly experienced and successful player in the lower divisions by the time he arrived at Elm Park in December 1989. His Football League career had started when he was spotted by Rotherham United playing as a part-timer for Bishop Auckland and working as a burner in the Swan Hunter shipyards on Tyneside.

He won a Division Three championship medal with Rotherham in 1980/81, then moved to Chesterfield and Peterborough United before joining Wolverhampton Wanderers, where he collected another Division Three medal as Wolves won the title in 1988/89.

When Ian Porterfield was desperate for a tough, combative midfield general to bolster Reading's flagging fortunes in 1989/90, he remembered Gooding's two-year spell at Millmoor under his management and had no hesitation in paying Wolves' asking price of £65,000.

Gooding already had over 400 first-class games under his belt, but his reputation as one of the fittest players in the professional game was maintained throughout his eight years with the Royals. He became a permanent fixture in midfield, never playing fewer then forty games a season and never giving less than the maximum effort.

He was a gritty competitor who hated to lose, and his dynamism rubbed off on the rest of the squad. The complete professional in every sense of the word, he was the key running midfield player around whom Mark McGhee built the side which won the Second Division in 1993/94 – enabling Gooding to earn his third championship medal.

When going forward he was lively, elusive and dangerous in front of goal, but his all-round tactical knowledge persuaded chairman John Madejski to appoint him as joint player-manager with Jimmy Quinn following Mark McGhee's sudden departure in December 1994. The two made the transition so smoothly that Reading's pattern of play was refined only marginally – but it was good enough to see the team reach the play-off at Wembley for a place in the Premiership. Gooding was distraught when Reading were beaten in

Mick Gooding was a regular goalscorer from midfield throughout his career with Reading. However, this goal, against Bradford City on 21 September 1991, could not save his team from a 2-1 defeat.

extra time, despite his own massive efforts as player and coach.

He completed two more seasons as player-manager, still battling away in the midfield hurly-burly and remaining one of the best players on the club's books; this was despite the fact that he was nearing forty and had many administrative tasks to undertake. His example helped keep the team in Division Two, but he was surprisingly released in the summer of 1997.

After a short spell out of the game he joined Southend United as player-coach, and made his 700th Football League appearance when he played as a substitute for them during the 1999/2000 season.

Gooding was called upon only briefly during the season, but was given the squad number 40 to match his age. During the current 2000/2001 season, he has become more used to passing on his knowledge to the younger players in the squad on the training pitch, though he is still registered as a non-contract player.

Len Grant
Right-back, 1921-1925

	First Team Appearances	Goals
Football League	77	1
FA Cup	2	0
FL Cup	0	0
Other	0	0
TOTAL	79	1

**LEN GRANT
CAPTAIN, READING F.C.
1923-24**

Reading's first England schoolboy international was Len Grant, who attended Battle School and was selected to play right half for his country against Wales at Walsall in 1907. He performed creditably in England's 3-1 win and the following season, at the request of the Reading Schools' committee, he played for the town team in a match at Elm Park, wearing his precious international cap! Not surprisingly, he showed a marked reluctance to head the ball whenever it came his way.

Len played in top-class local football after he left school and it was not until he was aged twenty-seven that he signed professional forms for Reading from Reading United. His wages at Elm Park were just £3 per week during the season and half that in the summer.

He made his debut, against Plymouth Argyle on 15 October 1921, at right-back and held his place for the rest of the season, scoring what was to prove his only first-class goal in a 1-1 draw at home to Portsmouth in the final game.

A series of injuries meant that he missed the whole of the next season, but he played in every game in 1923/24. He began at right-back again, but the arrival of Bert Eggo saw Grant move across to the left-back berth. At the end of the campaign he captained the Reading team which beat Brighton & Hove Albion 2-1 in the annual Royal Berkshire Hospital Charity Cup match at Elm Park.

A serious knee injury plus the arrival of Billy McConnell from Slough Town ended Grant's time at Elm Park. He never played football again and became the caretaker of G.R. Jackson's scrap-yard in Oxford Road. He still has a connection with Reading FC though, as his brother's grandson, Ron Grant, is the current kit manager for the club.

Dick Habbin
Utility player, 1969-1975

	First Team Appearances	Goals
Football League	219	42
FA Cup	14	3
FL Cup	14	4
Other	1	1
TOTAL	248	50

Dick Habbin first joined Reading on trial from Cambridge United in March 1969 after being spotted by manager Roy Bentley. However, it was Bentley's successor, Jack Mansell, who gave Habbin a professional contract and his debut against Doncaster Rovers on 6 September 1969.

Habbin fitted perfectly into Mansell's plans. He combined the role of a deep-lying centre forward with that of the target man who, despite his small stature, could control the ball tidily on his chest and provide openings for his fellow forwards. Reading topped the scoring charts for Division Three in his first season and in the Watney Cup tie against Manchester United Habbin netted Reading's first goal in a 2-3 defeat.

He headed Reading's goalscoring charts in 1971/72, but the next manager, Charlie Hurley, saw Habbin more as a midfield player and the goals began to dry up. He even played as an emergency right-back on occasions. This transition meant that his ability was never fully appreciated by the fans, and with his wife, Jenny, keen to get away from the area, Habbin applied for a transfer at the start of the 1974/75 season.

Reading were reluctant to let him go, but the Football League's independent tribunal set a fee of £35,000. This was the start of a long saga of appearances before the tribunal in London, until Habbin was finally sold to Rotherham United in February 1975 for only £10,000.

Curiously, Habbin totalled 47 League appearances for the 1974/75 season, adding 21 for Rotherham to the 26 he had already made for Reading. This would have been a Football League record, but for Geoff Barker adding 16 for Reading to the 34 he had already made for Darlington, to set a new landmark of 50.

Habbin spent two and a half seasons with Rotherham, then moved on to Doncaster Rovers for two more years. The latter clubs both used him as an orthodox centre forward and he repaid them both by getting amongst the goals once again. In his Football League career he played 340 matches, plus 22 as substitute, and scored 73 goals. He is now manager of Maltby Miners Welfare FC and the owner of a very successful building business.

	First Team Appearances	Goals
Football League	41	2
FA Cup	9	0
FL Cup	0	0
Other	0	0
TOTAL	50	2

Ted Hanney was born in Reading in 1889 and proved to be one of the finest players produced by the town. He began his football career with Wokingham Town and remained an amateur when he joined Reading in July 1910. He helped Reading to win the championship of the Southern League Second Division at the first attempt in 1910/11 and also starred in the club's thrilling FA Cup runs of 1911/12 and 1912/13. His excellence at centre half brought him selection for the England amateur international side which defeated Belgium and the Netherlands in 1912 and he also played for Great Britain in the 1912 Olympic Games held in Stockholm. He was centre half in the early rounds against Hungary and Finland, but missed Great Britain's 4-2 win over Denmark in the final because of injury.

Hanney also represented the Southern League and had played over 100 first team games for Reading before he was transferred to Manchester City for £1,250 – a massive sum in those days – in November 1913 and he went into their Football League Division One side. He was first choice at pivot for the next two seasons, but the First World War hampered his career with the Maine Road club. He moved to Coventry City in November 1919 for an even larger fee of £2,000 and played Second Division football for that club for two further seasons.

In July 1921 he returned to Reading to play one final season of League football. He captained the Biscuitmen, missing only one match as his team finished thirteenth in Division Three (South). At the end of that season he signed for Northfleet United in the Kent League, but soon hung up his boots to concentrate on coaching. He had a spell in Germany as coach of Stuttgart, but his heart belonged in his home town and he returned to Reading once more. He took over as licensee of the Russell Arms (now the Battle Inn) in the Oxford Road and combined that trade with the position of coach to the Berks & Bucks Football Association.

He was as thoughtful in his coaching duties as he was in his playing career, where every single appearance saw him placed at centre half. His style of play was composed and solid, yet always cultured and painstakingly correct. He eschewed the hefty boot into touch, preferring the well-placed pass to a colleague. He instilled the same values in those who were fortunate enough to come under his direction.

George Harris
Left-winger, 1966-1970

	First Team Appearances	Goals
Football League	136	57
FA Cup	11	4
FL Cup	9	5
Other	0	0
TOTAL	156	66

George Harris was one of those rarities in football: an orthodox, old-fashioned style winger who not only created chances for his colleagues in the forward line, but who also established a reputation as a consistent goalscorer himself.

Born in Lambeth, he played as an amateur for Woking, then scored regularly for Newport County and Watford in the lower divisions of the Football League. He joined Reading in the summer of 1966, at a time when Alf Ramsey had diminished the status of wingers, but George was employed as an outside-left by Roy Bentley and quickly repaid his manager. In his first season Harris scored 25 goals and in so doing broke the club record which had been set twenty-five years earlier by Ken Bainbridge.

He scored goals because he had pace, could time his jump perfectly to head the ball, read the game intelligently and was a reliable penalty-kick taker. He reached double figures in each of his first three seasons with Reading and was elected Player of the Season by the fans in the 1966/67 season.

Whether the team line-up included four or five forwards, he was always there in the wide-left position, either sending over accurate crosses for others to convert, or cutting in to snap up chances himself.

It was only when Jack Mansell took over from Bentley as manager in 1969 that Harris lost his place in the side and in October of that year he was transferred, together with Colin Meldrum, to Cambridge United for a joint fee of £4,000. He marked his debut for the Southern League club with a hat-trick in a 5-1 win against Nuneaton and regained his place in the Football League when Cambridge replaced Bradford Park Avenue in Division Four the following summer.

George Harris totalled 130 goals in 360 Football League games and in later years played for Rabsons Rovers in the Reading & District League.

Albert Hayhurst
Centre half, 1933-1939

	First Team Appearances	Goals
Football League	219	10
FA Cup	18	2
FL Cup	0	0
Other	10	0
TOTAL	247	12

Standing six feet tall and weighing just over thirteen stone, Albert Hayhurst had the ideal build for a stopper centre half. That role, however, was not his in the early days of his career. He preferred the forward line as a young player in his native Birdwell and joined Luton Town as a full-back. It was whilst playing for the latter club in a reserve game against Reading Reserves that Hayhurst's ability was noticed by manager Joe Smith and he signed Hayhurst on a free transfer during the 1933 close season.

Hayhurst had only made one Football League appearance for Luton, but he went straight into the Reading centre half and became the first name manager Smith wrote on the team-sheet each week. He missed only nine games in cup and League competition during his first five seasons with the club, and those were due to injury. He was as steady as the proverbial rock at the centre of the Biscuitmen's defence and the only criticism people made of his play was that he was too adventurous at times. He was described as more of a destructive than constructive player, one who excelled at breaking up opposing movements, rather than feeding his own forwards. He did, however, prove adept at moving upfield when Reading were awarded corner kicks or free kicks near the opposing goal and chipped in with a handful of vital strikes each season. He could recover his place in defence quickly, because although he was a hefty type, he was remarkably

agile and reputed to be one of the most assiduous trainers at the club.

Hayhurst was respected by opposing centre forwards for his clean and sporting demeanour on the field, and was the subject of several enquiries from First and Second Division clubs. But he stayed with Reading and won a Division Three (South) Cup winner's medal in 1938, when Reading defeated Bristol City in the final. Hayhurst switched from centre half to right-back, when Len Young arrived as pivot in December 1937. But he continued to give loyal service to Reading until injury ended his career. He played his last League game on 17 December 1938, away to Newport County.

Hayhurst, who spent his summers playing county cricket for Warwickshire, continued to live in Reading and as late as the 1980s could be seen strolling along the Oxford Road to do his shopping, meet neighbours, or call in for a haircut. He died, aged eighty-five, in 1991.

Stanley Hayward

Goalkeeper, 1875-1891

	First Team Appearances	Goals
Football League	0	0
FA Cup	14	0
FL Cup	0	0
Other	0	0
TOTAL	14	0

In Reading's early days as an amateur club, players were often required to fill any position in the team which might become vacant. A notable exponent of this versatility was Stanley Hayward, who made his debut for Reading as a half-back in 1875, but in a sixteen-season career played in every position for his side. His speciality was goalkeeping – in the days when the custodian guarded not a net but the open space between two posts and below a tape tied between them.

He was a consistent member of the team and played in every one of Reading's Berks & Bucks Cup games in the first twelve years of the competition, which had been instituted in 1877. He kept a clean sheet as Reading won the competition for the first time, defeating Marlow 1-0 at the Reading Cricket Club ground on 27 March 1879 and also prevented the opposition from scoring when Reading won their first FA Cup tie by beating South Norwood 2-0.

Newspaper reports of the day frequently referred to the expertise of the Reading goalkeeper. We are told that Hayward 'distinguished himself with his brave custodianship', that 'he saved expertly from a scrimmage in front of his goal', and that 'the play of Hayward between the posts could not be surpassed.' It was little surprise, therefore, that in addition to his games for Reading, he was also regularly selected for the Berkshire team, not only as goalkeeper, but also on occasions as full-back.

He remained an amateur throughout his time with Reading, which lasted until 1891, also serving on the club's committee and acting as secretary for a period. Additionally, he enjoyed a long and distinguished career in local government. Hayward served on the Reading Town Council for thirty-five years and was Mayor of Reading in 1918.

Stewart Henderson
Full-back, 1973-1983

	First Team Appearances	Goals
Football League	166	6
FA Cup	7	0
FL Cup	13	0
Other	0	0
TOTAL	186	6

Stewart Henderson was born in Bridge of Allan and was a Scottish schoolboy international in 1962. He came south to join Chelsea but never made it into their first team and was transferred to Brighton & Hove Albion in 1965 after an initial trial period.

He was to remain at the Goldstone ground for eight seasons and became a permanent fixture in either of the full-back positions, often opposing Reading. He was the club's Player of the Season in 1969/70, when Brighton just missed out on promotion from Division Three.

A free transfer brought him to Elm Park in June 1973 and he continued to give sterling service, usually at full-back. However, an inspired move by manager Charlie Hurley saw Henderson pushed into midfield and he responded by scoring twice in his first game there, a 3-1 victory at Bradford City.

When Maurice Evans took over as manager in 1977, he appointed Henderson as first team coach and it was expected that his playing career would end. Henderson had other ideas and remained fit by skippering the reserve team – often driving the minibus to games before getting changed to play – and he was recalled for occasional first team matches for another four seasons.

In 1983 he changed roles from coach to youth development officer and it was in this post that he did some of his most valuable work for the club. He had the knack of spotting good young players, as well as coaching, motivating and organising them – many of the Reading first team players of the 1980s and '90s owed their success to his patience and judgement.

As thoughtful and reliable in this part of his career as he had been as a player, Henderson finally left Elm Park in 1991. After eighteen years' loyal service to the Royals, he became youth team coach with Southampton FC.

Despite the many upheavals in the structure of the Saints, Henderson's integrity has ensured his survival at the Dell and he is approaching his tenth year of service with the club.

Les Henley

Wing-half, 1946-1953

	First Team Appearances	Goals
Football League	181	29
FA Cup	17	3
FL Cup	0	0
Other	0	0
TOTAL	**198**	**32**

Born in Lambeth in 1922, Les Henley represented South London Schools FA and was selected for the England Under 15 international team which met Scotland and Wales in 1937. When he left school he joined Margate, who were then Arsenal's nursery side, and played for them in the Southern League as a fifteen year old.

He failed to make Arsenal's pre-war first team and only played in one postwar FA Cup match. He was a regular in their Football Combination team though and during the war guested for several clubs, including Reading. When it became clear that his career was not going to progress at Highbury, he decided to return on a permanent basis to Elm Park and signed for Reading in 1947.

In his first four seasons at the club he played mainly at wing-half, but was converted to inside forward in time for the 1950/51 and 1951/52 campaigns, when Reading finished third then second in Division Three (South). A deep-lying inside man in the classical 'W' formation, he could score goals as well as provide openings for others.

In the latter of those two seasons he was a mainstay of the forward line, which was comprised of: Simpson, Edelston, Blackman, Henley, Bainbridge. Every one of those five forwards reached double figures as Reading accumulated 112 League goals – which is still a club record.

By now approaching the veteran stage, and after losing his place to younger players like Brooks and Parker, he moved to Ireland to take over as player-manager of Bohemians in 1953. He stayed for two years, then came back to England to be appointed as manager of Wimbledon in June 1955.

He stayed with the Dons for sixteen years, guiding them to three successive Isthmian League championship titles and an Amateur Cup triumph before entering the Southern League. He also led them to a Southern League Cup win in 1970 before resigning a year later.

Steve Hetzke

Utility player, 1971-1982

	First Team Appearances	Goals
Football League	261	23
FA Cup	11	1
FL Cup	28	5
Other	3	3
TOTAL	303	32

The potential of Steve Hetzke was noticed by scout Les Gaunt in 1970, and the youngster from Hungerford began to attend Tuesday evening coaching sessions under the guidance of manager Jack Mansell at Elm Park.

He progressed rapidly through the 'A' and Football Combination sides, and on 18 December 1971 played at centre-back against Darlington, aged sixteen years and 193 days. He thus became the youngest Reading player to appear in a Football League fixture – a record to this day. He steadily established his claim as first choice in the back four, despite a series of niggling injuries, and extended his experience by playing for Vancouver Whitecaps during the summer of 1976.

When Reading were desperate for goals he was moved into the forward line and spent the 1978/79 Division Four championship season as a converted striker, scoring 11 goals. Such was his versatility that he wore every first team outfield shirt except number 7, and was even the nominated emergency goalkeeper. It seemed inevitable he would be sold to a First Division club, but that never happened.

Despite captaining Reading in his last season with the club, Hetzke was placed on the transfer list in May 1982 and eventually sold to Blackpool for a tribunal-agreed fee of £12,500. It was a ridiculously low figure, for Hetzke also went on to captain his new side, playing to the same high standard he had achieved at Reading.

He later played for Sunderland, Chester City and Colchester United before ending his League career in 1990, the year the lattermost club were relegated to the GM Vauxhall Conference. He had played over 500 first team games and was widely recognised as one of the best defenders in the lower divisions.

Hetzke has made return visits to Reading in recent seasons as a monitor for the Football League, inspecting facilities at the Royals Academy.

Martin Hicks

Centre-back, 1977-1991

	First Team Appearances	Goals
Football League	500	23
FA Cup	39	1
FL Cup	38	2
Other	26	0
TOTAL	603	26

Generally agreed to be Reading's outstanding post-war player, Martin Hicks holds the club appearance record, with 603 first team appearances in all competitions. He is also the only Reading player to have won Division Three and Four Championship medals, as well as a Simod Cup winner's medal.

Despite this impressive record, his time at Elm Park was nearly over before it had begun. He joined the club from his home town Hellenic League side, Stratford Town, in 1975, but was released after a two month trial and was quickly snapped up by Charlton Athletic. He failed to make the grade there, and in February 1978 Maurice Evans paid £3,000 to bring him back to Reading.

So began his long and distinguished career with the Royals. He played in every game of the 1978/79 Division Four Championship campaign, when Reading set a Football League record of 1,103 minutes without conceding a goal. However, in the opening match of 1979/80 he sustained a serious ankle injury which sidelined him for over a year. In fact he suffered several horrendous injuries, including twice fracturing his jaw, as his bravery and spirit always saw him at the heart of any battle.

He was an inspirational skipper and captained Ian Branfoot's team, which set another Football League record by winning the first thirteen games of the 1985/86 season, and gained his Third Division Championship medal with that side. His proudest moment, however, arrived when he lifted the Simod Cup as Reading beat First Division Luton Town at Wembley in front of a crowd of 61,740, which included over 40,000 Reading fans. The 4-1 victory on 27 March 1988 was Reading's fifth over First Division opposition in the competition that season.

As a centre-back, Hicks was tall, commanding and composed, as well as being invaluable at set pieces in both penalty areas: many of his 26 goals came from towering headers at corners and free kicks. He more than compensated for any lack of finesse through strength and determination and led his team by example. The only surprise was that a bigger club did

Martin Hicks scores the first goal in a 3-0 win at Port Vale which clinched the Division Four championship for the 1978/79 season.

not attempt to sign him, but Martin was a loyal club man and an excellent advertisement for Reading FC both on and off the field.

He did eventually leave Reading, playing for Birmingham City for two seasons, from 1991 to 1993, then joined Newbury Town and Worcester City. He also appeared for an England Veterans XI, where he marked the great Pele, and, whilst working as a postman, the National Post Office XI.

Martin has now moved back to Stratford, but retains happy memories of his thirteen seasons at Elm Park. He often makes to the journey down from the Midlands to attend reunions, especially those of that marvellous Simod Cup team.

Skipper Hicks holds the Simod Cup aloft at Wembley.

Shaka Hislop

Goalkeeper, 1992-1995

	First Team Appearances	Goals
Football League	104	0
FA Cup	3	0
FL Cup	10	0
Other	9	0
TOTAL	126	0

Although born in London, Neil 'Shaka' Hislop was brought up in Trinidad, where he developed his love of sport and played in the same junior team as Dwight Yorke. He was also a talented fast bowler, but concentrated on his football when he studied in the United States. He completed a degree in mechanical engineering at Howard University in Washington DC and made a name for himself as the outstanding goalkeeper in college soccer.

He was brought to England by Reading manager Mark McGhee in 1992 and, after playing a handful of reserve games, made his debut against West Bromwich Albion on 9 September that year. He did not hold down a regular place, but in the following season, 1993/94, played in every first team match as Reading ran away with the Division Two title.

His goalkeeping skills had been honed by the coaching of former England 'keeper Peter Bonetti, and Hislop's enormous reach (he stood 6 feet 4 inches) and natural agility and anticipation, meant that he was becoming a target for Premier Division clubs. He remained at Elm Park for one more season, however, the 1994/95 campaign when Reading were within four minutes of reaching the Premiership themselves. Again Hislop was ever-present and his displays earned him not only the supporters' Player of the Season award, but also selection for the PFA Division One team.

The play-off final at Wembley was to be Hislop's last appearance for Reading. In August 1995 he was transferred to Premier giants Newcastle United for £1,575,000 – which is still the highest fee Reading have received for a player. He struggled with injuries for a while, but was called into the full England squad for training and was capped by the England Under 21 side as an over-age player against Switzerland in 1998.

In the summer of that year he moved again, this time to West Ham United. He established himself in the first team and is once again being tipped for England honours.

Johnny Holt

Centre half, 1898-1900

	First Team Appearances	Goals
Football League	0	0
FA Cup	2	0
FL Cup	0	0
Other	0	0
TOTAL	2	0

Although he had none of a centre-half's usual physical attributes, Johnny Holt was considered to be one of the outstanding pivots of his generation. He was only 5 feet 4 inches tall and weighed just 10 stones, but climbed the football ladder slowly yet steadily.

He began his career with junior clubs in and around his home town of Blackburn, then made his name and gained international recognition with Everton, whom he joined from Bootle in 1888. Whilst at Goodison he earned 9 England caps, a Football League Championship medal in 1891, and FA Cup runners-up medals in 1893 and 1897. He was apparently 'an artist in the perpetuation of minor fouls. When they were appealed for, his shocked look of innocence was side-splitting.'

Towards the end of his playing days he moved to Reading, arriving at Elm Park in October 1898. He was still proficient in the centre half berth, so much so that he was selected for his 10th and final England game, against Ireland in 1900, whilst played for the Biscuitmen – thus becoming the first Reading player to be capped for the full England side. He only made 29 competitive appearances for Reading and finished on the losing team just four times.

Throughout his playing days he was a noted exponent of the sliding, last-ditch tackle, and made a habit of appearing to scoop the ball to safety when a goal seemed inevitable. He retired immediately after the turn of the century and in 1902 was elected to the board of directors of Reading FC. Holt was unable to take up the post, however, as his application for reinstatement as an amateur was declined by the Football Association.

He later returned to the Liverpool area and just before the First World War was scouting for Reading. On one occasion he made an illegal approach to a player, causing Reading to be fined £30 and being censured himself.

Dean Horrix

Forward, 1983-1988

	First Team Appearances	Goals
Football League	158	35
FA Cup	9	4
FL Cup	12	1
Other	12	3
TOTAL	191	43

Although he was only twenty-eight when he died, Dean Horrix left an abundance of happy memories at the five Football League clubs for whom he played.

He was born in Taplow and played his early football on the park pitches of Slough before joining Millwall as an apprentice. He spent five seasons at the Den before moving to Gillingham in 1983, but his time at the Kent club was brief and unsuccessful, so he was transferred to Reading soon afterwards for £10,000.

He arrived at the same time as Trevor Senior and the two immediately formed a high-scoring partnership, with Horrix playing the role of the provider. During the peak of their time together, from 1983 to 1986, the duo plundered 136 goals. Horrix's share of the spoils was 37, plus countless assists. The duo were the scourge of the Third and Fourth Divisions and made the perfect striking combination, both being idolised by the South Bank fans.

Horrix particularly was the great entertainer, who played with magic in his feet and a twinkle in his eye. A tricky and intricate dribbler, his goals were special too. The dynamic shoulder-high volley, an extrovert step-over to dummy the goalkeeper in a one-on-one situation, or a clinically despatched penalty were his trademarks. Each one would be accompanied by a gleeful glance and a raised fist to the Royals supporters.

Out of favour towards the end of his five seasons with Reading, 'Deano' rejoined First Division-bound Millwall, then had a spell on loan at Cardiff City.

His final club was Bristol City, whom he joined in March 1990. It was while he was travelling home from only his third game for his new club that the car in which he was travelling hit a tree on the A340 near Tadley. Horrix was killed instantly.

At the next Reading home game, wreaths were laid in the centre circle and a minute's silence observed, as the crowd paid tribute to a remarkable talent that had been so cruelly extinguished.

George Johnson
Centre half, 1932-1937

	First Team Appearances	Goals
Football League	161	8
FA Cup	15	0
FL Cup	0	0
Other	3	0
TOTAL	179	8

George Johnson made his name originally as a free-scoring centre forward with Ashington, but failed to repeat that success when he moved into the Football League with Sheffield Wednesday. He played only one First Division game for the Yorkshire club, but scored in that match, a 4-0 victory over Blackpool in April 1931.

When he arrived at Elm Park in 1932, he was still considered a goalscorer and netted a hat-trick on his debut in a 4-0 win against Northampton Town on 17 December 1932. He only appeared twice more in that position, however, before being switched to right half by manager Joe Smith to plug a gap left by the departure of Len Darnell to Carlisle United.

It proved an inspired piece of thinking by manager Smith. Johnson was virtually ever-present for the next five seasons and captained the team. Reading never finished lower than fifth in Division Three (South) during those years.

He was the veteran in the team, a dour, tough competitor with a bone-crunching tackle, but who could also set up attacks with a variety of cogent passes. Despite his aggression he was seldom injured and the games he did miss were as a result of personal tragedy in his life, as he lost both his first wife and a daughter during his time with Reading.

He led his team into some epic FA Cup ties, notably against Arsenal and Manchester United, but remembered with great affection a tie against the gifted amateur club, Corinthians, at Elm Park on 30 November 1935. 'For twenty minutes they had us running round with our tongues hanging out', Johnson recalled, talking about the game almost fifty years later. But the skipper inspired his team to overcome the Corinthians' pace and enthusiasm, so that Reading finally won 8-3.

Smith's replacement as manager, Billy Butler, gave Johnson a free transfer in May 1937 and he moved to Watford, where he was re-employed in a goalscoring, forward role for two more seasons.

He returned to live quietly in Reading after the Second World War, and kept a house in Valentia Road until his death in 1985.

David Jones
Goalkeeper, 1953-1961

D. JONES *(Reading)*

	First Team Appearances	Goals
Football League	215	0
FA Cup	10	0
FL Cup	0	0
Other	9	0
TOTAL	234	0

Although he was born in Aberdare, David Jones moved to Kent while still very young and during World War Two was evacuated to Berkshire to escape Hitler's V-bombs. He began his goalkeeping career with Harwell in the North Berks League but signed professional forms for Brentford before being called up for National Service.

He spent three seasons with the London club without making a first team appearance before joining Reading in July 1953, and proved to be the most imaginative signing made by manager Jack Smith. He had to content himself with 'A' and reserve team football at first.

However, his natural goalkeeping skills were improved by the coaching he received from former Arsenal and Reading goalie George Marks. He forced his way into the first team and remained there for the next six seasons. He was an assured, calm goalkeeper, his specialities being the perfectly timed jump to catch a deep cross and the flying ballet-like save to hold an angled volley.

He reached his peak in 1958, when he was in the original forty-strong Welsh squad for the World Cup in Sweden. Jones never made the final twenty-two, however, and also missed out narrowly on selection for the Third Division (South) representative side.

In the 1961 close season, Jones left Reading for Aldershot and continued his League career for five more seasons. He played over 200 first team games for that club before retiring from professional football. He later became the games coach at Carmel College near Wallingford and is still a regular spectator at Reading's home games.

David also attends reunions of the former players, usually held at the Curzon Club each October. He always receives some good-natured ribbing from his pals. They always refer to the way in which he used to retrieve the ball from the net after conceding a goal. They all say that he would throw his cap on the ground and stand with his hands on his hips while looking around for someone to blame!

	First Team Appearances	Goals
Football League	145	36
FA Cup	10	6
FL Cup	11	1
Other	3	2
TOTAL	169	45

Born in Glasgow, Mike Kearney travelled south to begin his football career as an apprentice with Aston Villa, but returned to Scotland to play in junior football. His talent had not gone unnoticed by Maurice Evans, then managing Shrewsbury, and Kearney joined that club in 1972. Five seasons later he moved to Chester and eventually arrived at Elm Park in February 1978 for a fee of £10,000.

It was Evans who had signed him again and in his first full season with Reading, Kearney earned a Division Four championship medal as the club raced away with the title. All his appearances that season were as a front player, where he proved to be the perfect target man, able to control the ball with one touch, however it reached him. Not only could he create goals, he could score them too, and in 1979/80 top-scored with 16 strikes.

He returned briefly to Chester, but was signed for the third time by Maurice Evans, costing £50,000 on this occasion, and served Reading for three more years. Now he showed what a versatile footballer he was, as he moved to centre-back and held together an often shaky defence with his astute positional sense and combative interceptions.

Kearney's League career came to an end in

1983 after a series of injuries, though he continued to play local football for Reading Borough in the Sunday League. A broken leg finally decided him to finish playing and, in the tradition of several pre-war Reading footballers, he became a licensee, taking over the Horse & Jockey in Castle Street. He proved a popular landlord and revitalised the Royals Rendezvous when he moved to take charge there.

When Elm Park and the Rendezvous were demolished in 1998, Mike remained loyal to the club, and became manager of the promotions department at the Madejski Stadium. He retained a keen interest in local football as manager of Abbey Whitchurch, a leading Sunday League side.

Mike is always seen on the pitch at half-time during first team games, organising the Golden Gamble lottery draw.

Jack Lewis
Wing-half, 1951-1953

	First Team Appearances	Goals
Football League	74	17
FA Cup	7	0
FL Cup	0	0
Other	0	0
TOTAL	**81**	**17**

Wing-half Jack Lewis, whose proper name was John, was born in Walsall in 1919. He was on the books of West Bromwich Albion before the war, but made his Football League debut with Crystal Palace in April 1939. After the Second World War he was a regular in the Palace line-up and was right-half in their team which was beaten 10-2 by Reading on 4 September 1946. His personal form was good, however, and in 1948 he was selected for a London XI which played in Brussels.

In November 1949 he was transferred to Bournemouth for £7,500, then in the summer of 1951 he joined Reading, where he was to establish a Football League record. In 1951/52 Reading finished runners-up to Plymouth Argyle in Division Three (South). Disappointment at missing out on promotion was tempered by a club record of 112 Football League goals scored. Each of the five regular forwards reached double figures, as did Lewis, who played in all 46 games and was the team's penalty-kick expert. He was deadly from the spot, relying on force rather then finesse, producing an audible thud each time he hammered the heavy leather ball goalwards.

He scored twice against Crystal Palace on 5 April 1952, to equal Arthur Grimdell's record, set with Spurs thirty years previously, of 14 goals scored by a non-forward during a season. He now had seven games remaining in which to break the record, but had to wait until the fifty-ninth minute of the final match, at home to Bournemouth, for the opportunity. Denis Simpson was brought down in the area and Lewis thundered the ball into the net. His colleagues ran to congratulate him, and at full-time a spectator ran on the pitch and presented him with a bottle of champagne. This must have surprised Ron Blackman, who had netted the other four goals in Reading's 5-0 victory!

Lewis stayed with Reading for the 1952/53 season and was made captain, but had to wait until the final match of that season to score, as Ray Reeves had taken over as penalty-kick specialist. Lewis score twice from the twelve-yard mark in a 4-1 home win against Swindon on 1 May 1953 and that was to be his last game for the Biscuitmen.

He subsequently played for Southern League Kettering Town, and later became a publican in the Midlands, where his premises were often visited by Reading fans.

Stuart Lovell
Striker, 1990-1998

	First Team Appearances	Goals
Football League	227	58
FA Cup	16	2
FL Cup	13	5
Other	10	2
TOTAL	266	67

Stuart was born in Sydney, Australia in 1972 and moved to Reading when he was five. He attended Micklands Primary School, was selected for the Reading Primary Schools (under 11) team and cracked in 44 goals in 42 games for the representative side in the 1982/83 season. He was a natural goalscorer if ever there was one, and a keen Reading supporter too, who cheered on the Royals from the terraces during his teens.

He trained at Reading's Centre of Excellence from the age of eleven, and joined the club as a Youth Training Scheme player in 1988. In 1989/90 he was the leading scorer at Reading with 28 goals in reserve and youth team games, and was given his home debut the following season by manager Ian Porterfield. On 1 December 1990, he scored Reading's goal in the 1-0 win over Fulham, a date which was also memorable because it was the day when John Madejski took over as chairman of the club from Roger Smee.

Young Stuart must have impressed both manager and new owner, as he stayed in the first team for the remainder of the season and became a regular in Royals' strike force for the next eight years. He formed effective partnerships with a succession of front players.

His most productive campaign was in 1993/94, when he linked with Jimmy Quinn as Reading raced to the Division Two Championship. Lovell missed only one League match and totalled 20 goals whilst Quinn, to whom he had proved the perfect foil, amassed 35. Mark McGhee had taken over as manager by this time and must have had mixed feelings about the success of his young striker, for Lovell had told McGhee that the Scottish player-manager should drop himself in favour of Lovell.

The following season Reading experienced the trauma of reaching the Wembley play-off for a Premier Division place against Bolton Wanderers. Lovell's goals had done so much to get the club there, but he missed a penalty kick in the play-off final and Reading were beaten in extra time He has remarked on several occasions since that that miss will always stay with him. But he continued to be a

This is Stuart Lovell's second goal in a 2-0 home win against Stockport County on 28 December 1993.

loyal, hard-working and important member of the team and it was no little surprise when he was given a free transfer at the end of the 1997/98 season. He travelled north of the border to join Hibernian in the Scottish Premier League and has been a prominent member of their team ever since, although he tends to play a little deeper nowadays. He has also earned international selection for Australia.

Stuart was one of the most popular players to don a Reading shirt and had a great affinity with the South Bank crowd, who recognised him as one of their own. An intelligent player, nicknamed 'Archie' by youth team boss Bobby Williams, he had a full life outside football. He played in a rock band, did work experience with a local newspaper and was an excellent all-round sportsman. He was also a regular and popular attendee at supporters' functions. Hibernian's gain may well prove to be Reading's loss, for at a time when goalscorers are at a premium, Lovell has continued to find the back of the net for Hibs. His contribution has been material in assisting his new club to challenge Celtic and Rangers for the top spot in their division. His enjoyment of his new surroundings has been increased by the fact that he has also become a father for the first time.

	First Team Appearances	Goals
Football League	132	90
FA Cup	14	9
FL Cup	0	0
Other	5	5
TOTAL	151	104

One of the finest centre forwards in the club's history, Magnus 'Tony' MacPhee has been denied full recognition for his goalscoring exploits as most of his Elm Park career coincided with the Second World War.

Born in Edinburgh in 1914, he began his career with Belfast Celtic then moved across the Irish Sea to assist Workington in the North Eastern League. He spent a season with Bradford Park Avenue, then in May 1937 was transferred to Coventry City. He lost his finishing touch with the Midlands club and in June 1938 came south to sign for Reading for £2,750. He netted on his debut and ended the last peacetime season as leading scorer with 25 goals from 42 games. He also gained a Division Three (South) Cup winner's medal, scoring 4 times as Reading defeated Bristol City 6-2 on aggregate in the final held over from the previous season.

War intervened, although as MacPhee was employed in a reserved occupation he was able to play for Reading on a regular basis. He was Reading's leading scorer in each of the seven wartime seasons, totalling 216 goals. He was also a member of the Reading team which won the London War Cup, beating Brentford 3-2 at Stamford Bridge on 7 June 1941.

On the resumption of League football, MacPhee scored 8 goals in three games, including four in the record 10-2 win over Crystal Palace. He led the scoring charts in each of the first three post-war seasons before hanging up his boots in May 1949.

MacPhee's technique was interesting. As befits such an impressive goalscorer, he had a thunderous shot in both feet, but he rarely jumped for headers. He preferred to attack the ball from a standing start, arching his powerful neck muscles with both feet planted firmly on the ground. After retiring, he spent two years as assistant manager to Ted Drake and his success in developing young players for Reading enabled him to become manager of Walsall in July 1951. Although his brief spell in charge began brightly, results deteriorated and he resigned suddenly in February 1952, claiming that he had difficulty finding a house in the area.

MacPhee returned south and left football completely to take over the George Hotel at Basingstoke. Sadly his health worsened after he was involved in a car accident in Reading's Bath Road, and he was only forty-six years old when he died in 1960.

George Marks
Goalkeeper, 1948-1953

	First Team Appearances	Goals
Football League	118	0
FA Cup	8	0
FL Cup	0	0
Other	0	0
TOTAL	126	0

Born at Fighelden near Salisbury, George Marks was originally a carpenter. Standing only 5 ft 11 in tall, he was no giant of a goalkeeper and he played his early football for Salisbury Corinthians before being spotted by an Arsenal scout. He joined the London club in 1938 and made 2 appearances in their League team in the final pre-war football season. When the conflict started he displaced George Swindin as the club's first-choice 'keeper.

Marks played 8 times for England in wartime internationals, without winning a cap as none were presented whilst hostilities continued. He guested for several clubs, including Reading. RAF service saw him drafted abroad and when he returned from Europe Swindin had taken up permanent residence between the posts. Marks was transferred to Blackburn Rovers, where his former skipper Eddie Hapgood was manager, but two seasons later moved again.

He returned south to play for Bristol City, but that led to an even briefer sojourn of only 9 games. He finally came to Reading in exchange for Vic Barney and during the next five seasons shared goalkeeping duties with Jock McBride.

Very popular with the crowd, Marks was far from being a flashy last line of defence. He was a powerfully built and agile figure, with his black hair neatly Brylcreemed in the style of the time; he possessed a prodigious goal kick, was dominant in the air and brave in the box. His speciality was to pat down bullet-like drives then catch the ball to his stomach.

Marks suffered a bad injury in a friendly match against Rotherham United and finished playing in 1952. He coached at Elm Park for two years then returned to live back in Fighelden, whilst working for the government in Durrington. He had a leg amputated in 1996, entered a nursing home and then passed away in his sleep in 1998.

Billy McConnell
Left-back, 1924-1928

	First Team Appearances	Goals
Football League	142	1
FA Cup	20	0
FL Cup	0	0
Other	0	0
TOTAL	162	1

For almost seventy years Billy McConnell held the Reading club record as the most capped international player. He was also considered to be one of the most stylish players ever to appear in the club's colours and was one of the mainstays of the team that achieved so much in the mid-1920s.

He was born in Corbolis, but his family moved to Slough whilst he was young and he began his football career with amateur side Slough Town. His composed play at full-back attracted Reading's attention and he came to Elm Park in May 1924. He immediately made the left-back position his own and was first choice there for the next four seasons, until injury ended his career.

The hallmarks of his defensive play were tigerish yet immaculate tackling, long, raking passes out of defence and the ability to time his jump to win headers against taller opponents. He earned his first international cap for Northern Ireland against Wales in 1925 and stayed in the national side for the remainder of his time at Reading, winning 8 caps in total. His record was not eclipsed until Jimmy Quinn was capped, also by Northern Ireland, in 1994 for the ninth time. McConnell was also chosen for the Football League XI which met the Army FA in 1927.

McConnell's only goal for Reading came in the 2-1 home win over Middlesborough on 20 April 1927. He netted a last-minute winner, but broke his ankle in doing so and this was an injury from which he never fully recovered. He played for one more season, but retired in 1928 and took over the Lower Ship hotel in Duke Street.

He retained his interest in sport, often playing county cricket for Berkshire and Buckinghamshire, and subsequently moved back to Slough to run a newsagent's shop. He died, aged seventy-three, in 1974, after being admitted to hospital with further complications to the ankle injury which ended his footballing career.

Mark McGhee

Player- manager, 1991-1993

	First Team Appearances	Goals
Football League	45	7
FA Cup	1	0
FL Cup	2	0
Other	2	0
TOTAL	50	7

Mark McGhee played fewer than 50 Football League games for Reading, but his appointment as player-manager proved to be a masterstroke, as he built a side which won the Division Two Championship in 1993/94.

Although he was an untried manager before he arrived at Elm Park, McGhee had an excellent playing pedigree. The majority of his career had been spent with Scottish giants Glasgow Celtic and he had won a European Cup Winners' medal with Aberdeen. Additionally, he had gained 4 Scottish caps and been recommended for the Elm Park post by the Manchester United manager, Alex Ferguson.

Within a week of his arrival the youth team, under Bobby Williams, had won the Allied Counties Cup and League double, then McGhee saw his new team beat Stoke City 1-0 in the final game of the 1990/91 season. The close season saw him make some astute signings, including in particular Kevin Dillon. McGhee led the attack himself and, after some early reverses, the team finished in a respectable twelfth place.

Because of his contacts within the game, he could attract well-known players such as Jim Leighton and Steve Archibald, both Scottish internationals, to arrive on loan, but at the other end of the scale he was keen to encourage the younger players. Lea Barkus, Mark Holzman, Chris Seymour, David Bass and James Lambert were all given their opportunity and 1992/93 saw Reading improve to eighth place in the new Football League Second Division. McGhee finished playing at the end of that campaign and concentrated on management, assisted by Colin Lee. More bargain players arrived and the likes of Dylan Kerr, Jimmy Quinn and Ray Ranson all fitted smoothly into a side which raced away with the Division Two title. Playing exciting, attacking football, Reading headed the table in November and stayed there until May.

The following season promised even more success and Reading sought promotion to the Premier League. The club were on course for another championship, until McGhee left suddenly midway through the season to become manager at Leicester City. He left that club at short notice too and took over at Wolves. Unfortunately things did not go well and he was replaced by his coach at Reading, Colin Lee.

McGhee still lives in Reading and is often seen as a pundit on Sky Television. He was appointed manager of Millwall in September 2000.

Joe McGough
Inside forward, 1932-1938

	First Team Appearances	Goals
Football League	142	50
FA Cup	12	3
FL Cup	0	0
Other	5	1
TOTAL	159	54

One of Reading's most enthusiastic and reliable players during the 1930s was Joe McGough, who was born in Tow Law in 1909 and played his early football for a junior team called Middle Docks in the North. He was recommended to manager Joe Smith by a scout and arrived at Elm Park on trial in 1931.

He was not blessed with great physique – he was only 9 st 2 lb when he started with Reading, so Mr Smith told McGough to drink a bottle of Guinness each night to try and build up his strength. Smith would also go in goal to allow him extra shooting practice in the afternoons and McGough became a regular in the first team at inside-right in 1933, replacing Frank Eaton, who had been sold to Queens Park Rangers.

He was a tremendous asset to the team, not just for his own contribution but for the way in which he motivated his colleagues. He had limitless vitality and courage and excelled in the 'W' formation. At inside forward his play combined the creative skills of a goalmaker, with the covering and tackling of an abrasive defender. He was a consistent scorer, his best goal coming in a 3-1 win over Northampton Town when he ran from his own half of the field, beating all opponents, before slipping the ball into the net.

He could recall his years at Reading with great clarity almost half a century after he left the club. He told of the training schedule which saw the players have Mondays free, train at the ground on Tuesdays, play golf at Sonning on Wednesdays, train Thursdays, then do some sprints and have a rubdown from trainer Bill Clancy on Fridays. Some afternoons they would go for a walk in Prospect Park, then on Saturday afternoons, they would, in McGough's words, 'play like hell for two points and a £2 win bonus.'

McGough had digs at 2 Brisbane Road, where his landlady, Mrs Geandall, would give him a good luck kiss before he left for a home game and push a packet of cigarettes in his pocket. Trainer Clancy would give the players a sip of whisky before the game and at half-time, so they were well looked after!

McGough slips the ball into the net to score against Northampton Town on 10 April 1937.

He married a Reading girl in 1937 but was transferred to Chester for £500 in July 1938. He saw out his career there but retained his affection for Reading. Joe McGough was a marvellous character who made a great impression on all those who were fortunate enough to meet him.

When Reading played at Chester in 1980, McGough, who had continued to live in the town, arrived at the dressing-room on his bicycle. He went into the Visitors' dressing-room and introduced himself to all the Reading players as well as to manager Maurice Evans. His good will clearly had an effect, as Reading won the game 2-0, which must have produced mixed emotions for him.

When he learned that a history of Reading FC was being written, he sat down at home and wrote a fourteen page letter which told in fascinating detail of his time at the club. In that letter, his affection, not just for Reading Football Club but also for the town itself, became only too apparent.

Keith McPherson

Centre-back, 1990-1998

	First Team Appearances	Goals
Football League	256	8
FA Cup	12	0
FL Cup	20	1
Other	11	0
TOTAL	299	9

Keith McPherson had an ideal grounding as a professional footballer before he came to Reading. He began as a junior with West Ham United, who won the FA Youth Cup by beating Spurs in the 1981 final. He made one first team appearance for the Hammers, in a 0-3 home defeat against Liverpool on the last day of the 1984/85 season, but was loaned to Cambridge United to gain additional Football League experience. Thus prepared, he was transferred to Northampton Town in January 1986 for £15,000, and became a Cobblers first team regular until 1990. He played in every match as Northampton won the Division Four title with club record points. Besides being a first-class defender, his aerial power in the box often saw his name appear on the scoresheet.

After more than 200 games with Northampton, McPherson was sold to Reading for £100,000 in July 1990 as Ian Porterfield attempted to bolster an alarmingly porous defence. In his first season he formed a secure centre-back pairing with long-serving skipper Martin Hicks, but when Hicks left for Birmingham City, McPherson had to adjust to a series of new partners. He did so admirably and eventually combined with the young Adrian Williams to make the best central defensive unit in Division Two. Always keen to encourage and guide less experienced players, he was appointed club captain and kept that position throughout his the rest of his time with the Royals. He skippered both the side which won the Second Division championship in 1993/94 and in the following season, the team which reached the Division One play-off final at Wembley. In that game he played well and bravely, especially as he had to receive a pain-killing injection from club doctor Geoff Williams just before kick-off.

That was his style. Solid, sturdy and unspectacular, he marshalled Reading's defence, relying on his own brand of stubborness to be an example to his colleagues. Despite occasional absences through injury, he became one of a small number of players to make almost 300 first team appearances for the club.

At the end of the 1998/99 campaign he was given a free transfer, after a successful testimonial dinner had been held in his honour. He signed for Brighton & Hove Albion in the close season and extended his League career by another year. He joined Rymans Isthmian League club Slough Town in July 2000.

Colin Meldrum
Utility player, 1962-1970

	First Team Appearances	Goals
Football League	266	8
FA Cup	21	0
FL Cup	17	1
Other	0	0
TOTAL	304	9

Although he was born in Glasgow, Colin Meldrum moved south to join Arsenal as an apprentice in 1958. His appearances were limited to South East Counties and Metropolitan League football, so he switched to Watford in 1960 and made 32 League appearances for that club over the next two seasons.

Roy Bentley made probably his best signing when he brought Meldrum to Reading for just £1,500. The dour Scot proved to be one of the toughest, yet classiest, left-backs in the Third Division over the next five seasons and was only absent from the first team through injury.

He was an excellent motivator too, and could inspire all departments of his team with his powerful runs forward, which would frequently culminate in an accurate centre or a fiercely delivered shot to the far post.

After those years at left-back, he was moved into midfield by Bentley, where he continued to give equally committed performances each week and his goal tally began to accumulate. His sturdy frame enabled him to win a high proportion of the tackles he made and towards the end of his career at Reading he made an effective stopper in the centre-back position.

Meldrum failed to impress incoming manager Jack Mansell and moved to Cambridge United in 1969, where he had the distinction of scoring that club's first Football League goal in a 1-1 draw against Lincoln City. Despite captaining the League's newcomers, he returned to non-League football in 1971 with Hillingdon Borough.

After two more Football League games with Workington, he joined York City as trainer-coach in June 1973. He had a brief spell as caretaker-manager of the latter club in the 1980s, and was also manager of Workington for a short period.

	First Team Appearances	Goals
Football League	271	18
FA Cup	24	1
FL Cup	0	0
Other	0	0
TOTAL	295	19

Although Reading had several internationals on their books in the inter-war years, the best player to appear in their blue and white stripes during this time was almost certainly Alf Messer. He was second only to Bert Eggo in terms of games played, but he was also club captain from 1923 to 1930, a time when Reading won Division Three (South) and reached the FA Cup semi-final. Furthermore, he was recognised as one of the best centre-halves in England.

His career was ordinary to start with. Born at Deptford, South London in 1900, he began with the amateurs of Sutton United before moving to Mansfield Town, then Nottingham Forest without making a first team appearance for either club. It was only when he joined Reading in June 1923 that he began to realise his undoubted potential.

He spent half a season in the reserves being groomed as the successor to Eggo, both as centre half and captain, then made his debut against Luton Town on 15 December 1923. In the next six years he missed only two first team games and skippered the side throughout that period. He led his team to the Division Three (South) Championship in 1925/26 and to the FA Cup semi-final the following season.

As a centre half standing just over six feet tall, he was a brave, strong and resolute defender, at his best when he and his team had their backs to the wall. He never shirked a challenge, but he was something of a goalscorer and goalmaker as well and was tipped for international honours by the national press.

That recognition never came, but Messer was being watched closely by several leading clubs and it was no surprise when the directors decided to sell him, to Tottenham Hotspur, in July 1930 for a large fee. With his transfer went Reading's last hope of surviving in Division Two. He was an inspirational leader who had been described thus in the *Daily Mail*: 'Messer is the main cog in the Reading wheel, a creator of confidence, and the instigator of almost all the movements that lead to goals – he is the best man on the field.'

Messer spent four years with Spurs and

was appointed captain as soon as he arrived. He made his debut in a 7-1 win over Reading on 30 August 1930, at the start of a campaign which saw the Biscuitmen suffer many heavy defeats culminating in a return to Division Three (South). Messer stayed at White Hart Lane before a series of persistent injuries cost him his place and he moved to Bournemouth as player-coach in April 1934.

He subsequently returned to live in Reading and took over as landlord of the Truro public house in Castle Street, combining that job with coaching amateur club Oxford City. He died in Reading aged only forty-seven, on 28 July 1947. Alf Messer will always be remembered as the greatest centre half in the club's history.

Alf Messer follows Bert Eggo onto the field for Reading's first game of the 1926/27 season, away to Swansea Town.

Alf Messer, third from left, back row, pictured with the Reading team of 1925/26.

Gordon Neate

Utility player, 1958-1966

	First Team Appearances	Goals
Football League	99	2
FA Cup	5	0
FL Cup	2	0
Other	1	0
TOTAL	**107**	**2**

Currently Reading Football Club's longest serving employee, Gordon Neate joined the staff as an apprentice professional aged fifteen in April 1956. He had played football for Reading Boys and was such an outstanding local youngster that manager Harry Johnston had no hesitation in signing him as soon as he left Alfred Sutton School.

Gordon played in the minor and youth teams whilst working on the groundstaff and was a regular at centre half in the 'A' team that won Division Three of the Hampshire League in 1958/59. At the end of that season he made three appearances at full-back for the first team, his debut coming away to Colchester United on 20 April 1959. Over the next seven years he appeared in the Football League, Football Combination and Hampshire League sides, at either right-back, left-back or centre half. He could never be certain of a regular and uninterrupted run in the first eleven, partly because of the competition from other defenders but mainly due to a series of bad injuries. He made a total of 107 first team appearances, scoring twice, before retiring from playing full-time as a result of yet another serious knee injury.

The end of Gordon's playing career in 1966 coincided with the vacancy for a groundsman at Elm Park and despite having no formal training for the role, Gordon made an immediate success of the post. He assisted Bill Smith for a brief period, then took complete responsibility for preparing and maintaining the pitch, general ground maintenance and also making the perilous climb up and down the floodlight towers to replace the bulbs.

He continued to play local football for a while and also became a regular and popular performer in any charity matches in which he was invited to play. He even played in goal in a friendly match on the Sunday morning after his fiftieth birthday celebrations the previous evening! He loved Elm Park and his enjoyment and pride in working there was compounded by the fact that Viv, his wife, was the club's laundry lady and his son-in-law, Peter, played for Reading Reserves during the 1980s.

The closure of Elm Park in 1998 was a

sadder occasion for him than most, but he continues to serve Reading FC at the Madejski Stadium. Rewards for his loyalty have been few. He won a Football Combination Division Two championship medal in 1965/66, was presented with a Canon League Loyalty Award in 1985 and, in 1996, received the Football League Long Service Award – a unique distinction for a groundsman. One of the best-known characters in the town, admired for his ready wit and cheerful personality, Gordon intends to remain at the Madejski until he reaches retirement age in 2006. By then he will have completed half a century of service for his only football club.

Gordon Neate as groundsman.

Gordon, third from left, attempts to make an interception during a trial match at Elm Park in August 1964.

	First Team Appearances	Goals
Football League	59	54
FA Cup	7	0
FL Cup	0	0
Other	0	0
TOTAL	66	54

Although Jack Palethorpe only played 59 Football League games for Reading, he scored 54 goals, which makes him the player with the highest goals to games ratio for the club. His goalscoring potential had been clear from the start. He netted 65 times for amateur team Maidenhead United in 1929/30, then had a brief spell, still as an amateur, for Crystal Palace before joining Reading in May 1930. He scored regularly for Reading Reserves in his first season and in his first two appearances at centre forward in the Division Two side. But the management considered him too young at only twenty to lead the first team attack on a regular basis. Many fans believed that his goals would have saved the club from relegation but it was not to be.

The following campaign of 1931/32 saw Palethorpe score 23 goals in 28 Division Three (South) games, but he still could not be assured of a permanent place on the team. The following season he did even better, with 29 goals from 27 starts. Such marksmanship did not go unnoticed and he was sold to Stoke City in March 1933 for the considerable sum of £2,000. He scored the goal that won Stoke promotion, then repeated the feat with his next club, Preston North End.

But his greatest triumph was still to come. In December 1934 he moved again, to Sheffield Wednesday. His goalscoring enabled the Yorkshire club to finish third in Division One, but he also scored in four of the six rounds as Wednesday won the FA Cup. In the final at Wembley, he netted after only two minutes and settled nerves as they romped to a 4-2 win over West Bromwich Albion.

Despite this, he fell out of favour surprisingly quickly. By November 1935 Aston Villa had signed him, in a vain attempt to avoid relegation to Division Two. He returned to Crystal Palace for a time, then signed for Chelmsford City as they entered the Southern League in 1938. He continued to rattle in goals, and helped Chelmsford defeat League opposition Darlington and Southampton to reach the fourth round of the FA Cup. He played for Shorts Sports when the Southern League was suspended in 1939.

Popular with his colleagues wherever he played, Jack Palethorpe was a natural goalscorer, and a dressing-room comic who never let disappointments spoil his love of the game. Jack's nephew, Chris, also joined Reading from Maidenhead United in the early 1960s. Jack died in May 1984 at the age of seventy-four.

Phil Parkinson

Midfielder, 1992-present

	First Team Appearances	Goals
Football League	279	14
FA Cup	18	1
FL Cup	24	2
Other	9	0
TOTAL	330	17

Midfield dynamo, club captain, academy coach and team manager, PFA delegate, Open University student – all of these descriptions fit Phil Parkinson. Moreover, he has a far greater rapport with the Reading fans than most of his contemporaries or predecessors.

Phil has been at the club since 1992. Before that he had left his home town of Chorley to become an apprentice at Southampton. He was unable to gain first team recognition at The Dell and was bought by Bury for £13,000 in the close season of 1988. He stayed with the Shakers for four seasons, during which he played 145 Football League matches as a tough tackling midfield player, scoring 5 goals. Bury were relegated in his last season at the club and he was transferred to Reading for the bargain fee of £37,500 in July 1992.

It was an astute piece of business by Mark McGhee. He knew that he had to add steel to the creativity already evident in his side and Parkinson was just the player to do that. He was the workhorse who had to win the ball in the tough midfield battles of Division Two so that other members of the team could show their skills. He did his job to perfection, his robust and abrasive technique making sure that Royals enjoyed enough possession to play the majority of the game in the opponents' half of the field.

He fully deserved his Division Two championship medal of 1993/94 and explained at the end of the season that manager McGhee and coach Colin Lee had helped to make him a far better and more aware player than he had been previously.

His game is about much more than mere ball-winning, however. Totally committed to the cause of the side, he is an excellent example to aspiring youngsters: not only does he train and play to his utmost ability, he has done what so few professional footballers remember to do and he has prepared for when the time comes to stop playing.

Phil is studying for an Open University Bachelor of Science degree in Sociology. It is difficult to fit in homework with the ever-increasing demands of the modern game, but he is as dedicated off the field as he is on it. He also finds time to coach at the Royals

Phil Parkinson heads Reading's second goal in a 4-1 home win against Barnet during the 1993/94 championship season.

Academy and manage their team, which plays on Sunday mornings. As if that is not enough, he is the Professional Footballers' Association representative at Reading FC and sometimes called on to arbitrate in disputes between players and management.

He has been with Reading for eight seasons now and although his battle scars are beginning to have an effect, he will soon move into the top ten of appearance makers for the club. When the time comes to hang up his boots, the fans, with whom he has always enjoyed mutual respect, will hope that remains with Reading FC in a post where he can pass on his expertise and enthusiasm.

During the 2000/2001 season, Phil has kept his regular place in midfield, despite tough opposition from new signings and improving youngsters, and is playing as well as ever. Nevertheless, he is making additional provision for his future by studying for his UEFA 'A' Coaching Licence.

Gary Peters
Right-back, 1975-1979, 1984-1988

	First Team Appearances	Goals
Football League	256	11
FA Cup	15	0
FL Cup	21	1
Other	2	0
TOTAL	294	12

Although he made a comparatively late entry to the professional game, Gary Peters had a remarkably successful career with lower division clubs, especially Reading. Whilst with the Royals he played in one promoted team, two championship-winning sides and came on as substitute for Reading when they won the Simod Cup at Wembley.

He was spotted by Charlie Hurley playing for Guildford City, came on trial in March 1975 and signed for a small fee two months later. He was the regular right-back in the side which won promotion to Division Three in 1975/76, experienced relegation the following season, then missed only one game as Reading won the Division Four title in 1978/79. His clearance off the line in a 3-0 win at Port Vale enabled Reading to set a Football League record of 1,103 minutes without conceding a goal.

Failure to agree terms meant that he moved to Fulham for £25,000 before the start of the new season, then in 1982 he moved again, this time

to Wimbledon. He captained that team to promotion to Division Two before joining Aldershot.

Peters returned to Reading in March 1985 on a free transfer, ostensibly to captain and educate the young reserve team. Such was his dedication, however, that he forced his way back into the first team and won his second championship medal with Reading as Ian Branfoot's team ran away with the Division Three title in 1985/86. Although in the veteran phase of his career by now, he was still the perfectionist in training as well as matches and could produce immaculate displays either at the back, in midfield, or on his occasional forays up front.

The ultimate competitor, his challenges were as abrasive on the practice pitch as anywhere, but his team-mates loved him for his boundless enthusiasm. First team appearances diminished as he grew older and he made a sentimental farewell to the club. In one of his last games for Reading he replaced Mick Tait in the 83rd minute as the Royals beat Luton Town 4-1 in the Simod Cup final at Wembley in March 1988.

Gary ran the Blue Lion pub at Bracknell for a while, then went into coaching and management, firstly with Cambridge United and then more recently with Preston North End.

Jimmy Quinn

Striker, player-manager, 1992-1997

	First Team Appearances	Goals
Football League	182	71
FA Cup	9	5
FL Cup	16	12
Other	9	6
TOTAL	216	94

When Jimmy Quinn was signed by Mark McGhee from AFC Bournemouth for £50,000 in the summer of 1992, it is doubtful if he realised he was bringing to Elm Park a player who would replace him as manager as well as main striker.

But McGhee should have been warned. Although Quinn was a late developer, having begun his working life as a gents' outfitter at Debenham's in Croydon, his professional career had an outstanding pedigree and he was a proven goalscorer. He had played for Swindon, Blackburn, Leicester, Bradford City and West Ham before Bournemouth and was also a regular in the Northern Ireland side. He led the scorers in his first season with the Royals and added an extra dimension to the team with his bullet-like heading and exquisite first touch, which could bring so many colleagues into the game.

The following season, 1993/94, saw him at his most prolific, as he scored 35 goals in 46 League games whilst leading Reading to the Second Division championship. He had a thunderbolt shot in both feet and his penalty kicks threatened to go straight through the goalkeeper. He was also a more than competent emergency goalie himself.

In 1994/95 he took over as joint player-manager with Mick Gooding after the sudden and unexpected departure of McGhee. The two of them continued to play regularly and refined the playing system to the extent that Reading qualified for the Premiership play-off against Bolton Wanderers at Wembley. Quinn scored in extra time, but it was not enough as Reading went down 3-4.

He remained at Elm Park for two more seasons, leading the team in a desperate fight against relegation on both occasions as members of the play-off squad departed. Quinn's goals did much to keep Reading up and his second strike in a 3-0 win over McGhee's Wolves – when he turned, juggled the ball and flicked it up for a crashing volley – was the best seen at Elm Park for many seasons.

More of a motivator and a cajoler than a tactician, and one who led very much by personal example, Quinn's contract was

Quinn heads Reading's first goal in a 3-0 win over Northampton Town on 18 August 1993.

not renewed at the end of the 1996/97 campaign. He joined Peterborough United, then took over at Swindon Town as manager in 1999 in difficult circumstances. That appointment lasted less than a year, but he did return to Wembley, playing at centre forward for the Hungerford Veterans team that won the Umbro Cup.

Jimmy Quinn is the most-capped Reading player, making 17 international appearances for Northern Ireland and scoring 6 goals during his time with the Royals.

Although now aged 41, Jimmy Quinn is still playing and scoring goals. Since leaving Swindon Town, he has turned out for Cirencester, Northwich Victoria and Hereford United. Most recently he has signed for Highworth Town of the Hellenic League, and combines his football with a business in Swindon.

	First Team Appearances	Goals
Football League	284	28
FA Cup	22	2
FL Cup	0	0
Other	11	1
TOTAL	317	31

By reputation at least, Ray Reeves is considered to be the player with the hardest shot in the history of Reading Football Club. The nickname of 'Bomber' was an apt one to apply to the well-built full-back, who weighed in at thirteen stone and stood six foot tall. He was a great favourite with the Elm Park crowd, who enjoyed the way he used his powerful physique to control opposing wingers and thunder ferocious long range clearances down field.

He was born in Reading and during a successful youth career played for an FA Youth XI in Holland, also representing Berks & Bucks in the FA County Youth Championship. He signed for Reading as a groundstaff junior in 1947 and graduated through the club's minor, youth and reserve sides to make his first team debut away to Shrewsbury Town on 29 November 1952. He played at left-back, thus enabling Stan Wicks to move to centre half, and he remained a regular in that position for the next nine seasons. Sometimes he was selected at centre half himself and, occasionally, if the team were losing, he would be pushed upfield to lend his not inconsiderable weight to the attack. He totalled 31 goals for the club, 22 of them from the penalty spot and most of the remainder as a result of free kicks, which he struck with tremendous velocity from outside the area. The opponents' crossbar literally shuddered on occasions when his shooting was marginally off target. But he was a more than competent defender too, and frequently used his massive frame to block goal-bound shots when his own 'keeper had been beaten.

'Bomber' played over 300 games for Reading, captaining the team for several seasons, before being transferred to Brentford in 1961. He played mainly in the London team's Football Combination side, and added just 5 League appearances to the total he had amassed with Reading. He retired from full-time football, but continued to play as a part-timer with Dover, then Burton Albion, in the Southern League. When he finished playing he returned to Reading to manage a dairy and play in occasional friendly and charity matches.

Now retired and living in Buckingham Drive at Caversham, his sporting activity is confined to a game of bowls for the Island Bowling Club, but he regularly attends the reunions of former Reading players held each October.

Frank Richardson

Centre forward, 1926-1930

	First Team Appearances	Goals
Football League	91	44
FA Cup	12	11
FL Cup	0	0
Other	0	0
TOTAL	103	55

Although Frank Richardson's career with Reading was relatively brief, it was highly successful. He was bought from Swindon Town in February 1926 as the final part in the jigsaw which would enable the Biscuitmen to be promoted to Division Two, and his twelve goals in the final thirteen League games ensured the Championship.

He was born in Barking in 1897 and played amateur football for that club before turning professional with Plymouth Argyle in 1921. He made an immediate impact, finishing that season as leading scorer in Division Three (South) with 31 League goals. He aroused the interest of other clubs, but never reproduced comparable form in subsequent moves to Stoke City, West Ham and Swindon Town.

It was only when he was transferred to Reading that the goals began to flow once again and the stocky centre forward crashed home the goals which took Reading near the top of the division. In the final game, at home to Brentford, Reading needed to win to be certain of going up. Richardson obliged by scoring four times, including a penalty, in a 7-1 victory that saw the team crowned as champions. He stayed at Elm Park for four more seasons, remembering the highlight of those years as the run to the FA Cup semi-final in 1926/27, when he netted nine goals in ten matches. He rejoined Swindon Town in 1930, but never moved away from Reading.

His style of play was simple. He would run on to crosses or through balls and smash the ball at goal with either foot. He timed his jumps and headed the ball to perfection and his close-range headers were as powerful as some players' shots. He was deadly accurate and respected by opponents as a hard but fair competitor.

Frank left professional football in 1935 to work in the Reading Borough Treasurer's office and lived alone in a bedsitter in Oxford Road, He returned to Elm Park in the mid-1950s to coach the youth team, but retired in 1966. He made an emotional farewell to the club on 5 May 1986, when he was brought onto the pitch in his wheelchair to help celebrate Reading's 2-0 home win over Doncaster Rovers and the championship of Division Three. Although clearly very frail, he waved his stick vigorously at the supporters and signed several autographs, though each one required considerable effort. He died peacefully a year later, aged ninety.

	First Team Appearances	Goals
Football League	380	3
FA Cup	32	0
FL Cup	26	0
Other	19	0
TOTAL	457	3

Steve Richardson was born in Slough and was an outstanding schoolboy athlete. He played soccer for the Slough Schools teams at all age levels and also represented Berkshire Under-15s. He was a county champion sprinter and reached the finals of the English Schools one hundred metres championship.

He was scouted by Southampton and joined as an apprentice when he left school, but although he spent four years at the Dell he was unable to break into the first team. He won a Football Combination championship medal in 1980/81 and was on the bench for an UEFA Cup tie against Sporting Lisbon, but a free transfer to Reading saw him pitched into immediate Football League action.

It was the start of a ten-year career with the Royals which saw him rarely displaced from the first team and he participated in many highs and lows during that time. Relegation in his first season was followed by promotion in the next and in 1985/86 he was a regular in that marvellous team of Ian Branfoot's that stormed to the championship of Division Three after setting a Football League record by winning their first thirteen games. Relegation came again in 1987/88, but was compensated for by the Simod Cup win at Wembley, where he gave an outstanding performance at left-back.

Steve totalled over 400 first team games for the club, one of only eight players to do so, and scored 3 goals, all away from home. Two of them earned Reading draws, 3-3 at Orient on a Sunday morning, and 1-1 at Ipswich on the last day of the 1986/87 season, a result which meant that the Royals finished 13th in Division Two. At the time that was the club's best performance in the Football League.

At left-back, where he played for a decade, Steve Richardson used his pace to good effect. When he was beaten he could recover and get back in position for a second attempt at a tackle. He covered, harried and chased and the poor games he played could be counted on the fingers of one hand. Surely he was one of the best free transfer signings ever, certainly in the history of Reading FC.

When he left the club in 1993 he joined Newbury Town, then moved to Basingstoke Town, where he skippered the Isthmian League side. He combined part-time football with his business as a painter and decorator.

Lawrie Sanchez
Midfielder, 1977-1985

	First Team Appearances	Goals
Football League	262	28
FA Cup	14	1
FL Cup	22	0
Other	7	2
TOTAL	305	31

Selection for the Reading Primary Schools Under 11 team as a nine-year-old gave Lawrie Sanchez's football career an encouraging start and he showed early potential as he progressed through the district and Berkshire county age groups. At sixteen he was playing regularly for Thatcham Town in the Hellenic League and in 1977, made his debut for Reading in a Division Four game against Wimbledon while still studying for his 'A' levels. On 22 October 1977, on his eighteenth birthday, he scored his first League goal in a 2-0 home win over Crewe Alexandra.

Having gained 13 'O' levels and 4 'A's, he entered Loughborough University, but not before he had represented the England Schools Under 18 team twice in international matches against Scotland. Whilst at Loughborough, where he gained a BSc. degree in Business Management, he continued to play for Reading's first team, thus becoming the first professional footballer to take up full-time further education and stay in the game.

Lawrie's style of play as a quality midfielder was deceptively casual. He had elegance and assertiveness and his passing ability was frequently too advanced for some colleagues. He won a Division Four championship medal with Reading in 1978/79, but his most notable successes came after he left Elm Park. He seemed destined to join Swindon Town in December 1984, but instead was sold to Wimbledon for £25,000. He became an automatic choice for the Dons, scored the goal which gained them promotion to Division One, and, on 14 May 1988, headed the only goal of the game as Wimbledon beat Liverpool 1-0 in the FA Cup final, one of the greatest upsets in the competition's history.

He stayed at Wimbledon for nine seasons, while he also won 3 caps for Northern Ireland, then played a handful of games for Swindon before moving into management. He became player-manager of Sligo Rovers before returning to England to coach the Wimbledon reserve side to the Football Combination championship. He progressed further up the ladder when he was appointed manager of Second Division Wycombe Wanderers in 1999 and made an immediate impact by saving the club from relegation. A combination of sharp intellect, good experience and excellent coaching ability means that he is one of the best young managers in today's game.

	First Team Appearances	Goals
Football League	301	154
FA Cup	32	18
FL Cup	17	14
Other	12	5
TOTAL	362	191

Not only the greatest goalscorer in the club's history, but a dedicated trainer, true sportsman and perfect gentleman on and off the pitch, Trevor Senior was a manager's dream.

Born in a pub in Dorchester, he made his name with his home town non-League club before joining Portsmouth for £20,000 in 1982. He scored his only 2 League goals for the South Coast club against Reading before being loaned to Aldershot, where he netted 7 goals in 10 matches towards the end of 1982/83. His promise had been noted by Maurice Evans, who brought him to Elm Park in the summer of 1983 for £35,000 as the natural replacement for Kerry Dixon.

As soon as Senior arrived he began to set goalscoring records. In his first home League game he completed a hat-trick in four minutes during a 6-2 win over Stockport County. By the end of the season he had totalled 41 goals in all competitions to beat Ron Blackman's record, which had stood for thirty-one years. He became the first Reading player to top the Football League goalscorers and won a PFA Division Four medal as well as a Rothmans Golden Boot award.

The goals continued to flow and in the following season of 1984/85 he netted in nine consecutive matches to break Alf Bacon's fifty-five-year-old record. A season later and

he was leading scorer in Ian Branfoot's marvellous all-action team that ran away with the Division Three title.

Senior made goalscoring look simple, yet he was an amazingly hard worker, who did his share of defending at the near post or marking the opposing centre-back when occasions demanded. His goalscoring technique consisted of timing his run to perfection so that he arrived unmarked in the area, then hitting the ball low and early. Rarely did he take more than one or two touches before netting and he seemed to score with various parts of his body. He was respected by opponents for scrupulously fair play and won another PFA Divisional medal in 1985/86 to go with his championship medal.

After a season in Division Two he joined Watford for £300,000 and also played briefly for Middlesborough before returning to Elm Park in October 1988. Still the goals came and he was the leading scorer for each of the

Trevor Senior heads a goal for Reading in an FA Cup tie against Arsenal. Despite his efforts, Reading were beaten 3-1 on 10 January 1987.

next three seasons as Reading returned to Division Three.

Trevor was also a more-than-competent emergency goalkeeper and went between the posts on four occasions in League games without conceding a goal, the last occasion being his final appearance for Reading in a 3-2 win against Wigan on 2 May 1992. The fans chaired him from the pitch at the end of the game.

Great mutual respect and admiration existed between Senior and Royal's fans, and he was always keen to support their events. He played for Woking, then returned to Dorchester and became player-manager of Bridport Town in the Western League. More recently he has been coaching Bashley.

Trevor's love for the game remains constant, as does his affinity with the town of Reading. He returns regularly to play in charity matches and to visit old friends. He was runner-up to Robin Friday in the Reading FC 'Player of the Millenium' vote which was organised by the club in December 1999. He attended the dinner at the Madejski Stadium when he was presented with his award.

Roger Smee

Striker, 1966-1970, 1973-1974

	First Team Appearances	Goals
Football League	59	17
FA Cup	5	0
FL Cup	2	0
Other	0	0
TOTAL	66	17

Although Roger Smee never claimed a regular place in the Reading first team line-up, his contribution to the club was a major one and without it there would be no Reading Football Club today.

His playing career was brief and unspectacular. A pupil at Forest School, Winnersh, he joined Chelsea as a schoolboy and after being released by the London club joined Reading. For four seasons he made intermittent appearances as a striker, scoring goals at widely spaced intervals. He moved into non-League football with Chelmsford City, then made a short comeback with Reading during the 1973/74 campaign. That was ended by injury and again non-League football beckoned and he ended his playing days with Hereford United then Hillingdon Borough.

Smee now concentrated on his business interests, becoming chairman of the Rockfort Group and when Reading FC was put up for sale in 1983 he seemed the ideal person to take over. His first bid was rejected, but when Robert Maxwell threatened to merge Reading and Oxford United to form Thames Valley Royals, Smee led the fight against the proposed takeover. Assisted by directors Jim Brooks and Roy Tranter, as well as a vast groundswell of public opinion, his efforts proved successful and Maxwell's proposed merger, which would have meant the closure of Elm Park, never happened.

Smee became chairman of Reading FC, replacing Frank Waller, and it was during his time in charge of the club that manager Ian Branfoot's team won the Division Three championship for the 1985/86 season. His tenure as chairman ended in 1990, when he was replaced by John Madejski, but he continues his interest in the property and building business to this day.

Herbert Smith
Left-back, 1902-1910

	First Team Appearances	Goals
Football League	0	0
FA Cup	16	0
FL Cup	0	0
Other	0	0
TOTAL	16	0

Born at Witney in Oxfordshire in 1879, Herbert Smith is one of Reading's greatest players. Despite the fact that he never became a professional, he remains the club's most capped England international. He played for a number of teams, including Oxford County and Beccles Schools, Oxford City, Witney, Richmond, Clapton and Stoke City before joining Reading in 1902, six years after the Biscuitmen had moved to Elm Park. He made 14 appearances for the England amateur team, including two as captain, and assisted the Great Britain team which won the 1908 Olympic gold medal.

He played 4 times for the full England team, against Wales (twice), Scotland and Ireland – and was never on the losing side. In the game against Scotland, in which he began the move that led to England's goal in a 1-0 victory, his performance was described thus by *Football Chat*: 'Smith was the best back on the field on Saturday, and surely that is praise in such company. He had the happy knack of doing the right thing at the right time. His success was even greater on account of having such a strong wing against him.' Smith also captained Oxford City to the Amateur Cup final in 1903, which they lost after a draw at Elm Park.

With Reading, Smith was a regular member of the Southern League team which achieved much success in the early 1900s and frequently captained the side, despite being the only amateur in the line-up. He played at left-back and was described as a burly but scrupulously fair defender, whose dextrous left foot was almost legendary. He possessed an excellent physique and combined the qualities of speed, skill and precise distribution.

According to the 1906 *Book of Football*, his reputation wase partly due to his abstinence. In his introduction to the Reading Schools Football Association's handbook for 1907, he said, 'A great thing for boys who intend to take football seriously is to leave all intoxicating drinks severely alone. Smoking interferes with the wind, and this as we all know, must be in good condition if we are to play a hard game of football. In conclusion, I would advise all boys to "play the game" for all it is worth, whether you are winning or losing. Besides, "playing the game of football" teaches us to "play the game of life."'

Such was the philosophy of this true amateur who represented all that was good in football. Fittingly, Smith was elected President of the Oxfordshire Football Association on retirement, a post he held until his death in 1951.

Herbert Smith (white shirt) in action for England against Scotland at the Crystal Palace on 1 April 1905.

Herbert Smith.   Mr. J. R. Blandford,   J. Bainbridge,   S. Higginson,   J. Long.   E. Gettins,   M. Allman,   Mr. J. B. Messer,
(Captain.)   W. Garbutt,   H. Devlin,   Photo. Everard Cusner, Rea

Herbert Smith pictured as an insert on the Reading team photograph for the 1905/06 season. Smith is wearing his England international jersey.

Dick Spiers
Centre half, 1955-1970

	First Team Appearances	Goals
Football League	453	3
FA Cup	27	1
FL Cup	20	0
Other	5	0
TOTAL	505	4

Dick Spiers is one of only three players (the others being Steve Death and Martin Hicks) to have made over 500 first team appearances for Reading. Born in Benson, Oxfordshire he began his playing career with Cholsey United before joining Reading as an amateur, finally signing professional forms in October 1955. For most of the 1955/56 season he played at centre half for the Reading 'A' team that finished bottom of the Hampshire League Division One and, although his defence was under frequent pressure, he spent the time learning his trade as a tough yet cultured stopper.

Next came National Service with the Oxon & Bucks Light Infantry and the opportunity to play for the full Army XI, alongside such well-known international stars as Bobby Charlton, Duncan Edwards and Cliff Jones. He was able to return to Reading for occasional appearances in the first team when not required for military duties, but for several seasons had to share the centre half duties with the more experienced Bill Davies. By 1960, however, he had established himself as first choice and in a spell of five seasons, from 1961 to 1966, he missed only four games in the number five shirt – a remarkably consistent record.

Goalscoring did not come quite so easily and Spiers managed only 4 goals throughout his fifteen seasons at Elm Park. One of these was a vital equaliser in an FA Cup tie against Newport County and one came in his final appearance in a Reading shirt – a 3-1 home win over Stockport County on 13 December 1969. He also scored in his well-supported testimonial match against West Ham United at the end of that season.

After leaving Reading in the summer of 1970, Spiers played for Banbury United in the Southern League, where he continued to take part in the kind of physical battles much relished by centre halves in the lower divisions. He had set up his own joinery business in Benson whilst with Reading and that became his main interest once he finished playing. He did, however, act as a scout for some years for Reading, though his son, Alan, an England schoolboy

Dick Spiers jumps to head a goal in the FA Cup tie against Newport County on 9 January 1965.

international, joined West Ham after leaving school.

Dick Spiers will be recalled as a strong, sturdy and dependable centre half, who was effective rather than spectacular. Not especially powerfully built, but with a wiry physique which enabled him to compete with the roughest of centre forwards, he became a firm favourite with local supporters. He attended the reunion of former Reading players held at the Curzon Club in Oxford Road two days before his death, aged sixty-two, on 22 October 2000.

At Dick's funeral in Benson parish church, many tributes were paid to a man who had lived a very full life. Friends recalled his love of the countryside and his pride in his family. Also on show, although he himself would have been far too modest to display them, were souvenirs from his time in football, including home and away Reading programmes, letters confirming his selection for the Army Football Association teams, and photographs of his school and youth teams. It was a moving occasion in memory of one of the finest players ever to wear a Reading shirt.

Tommy Tait
Centre forward, 1934-1939

	First Team Appearances	Goals
Football League	144	79
FA Cup	15	14
FL Cup	0	0
Other	9	10
TOTAL	168	103

Although Tommy Tait was only twenty-six when he joined Reading from Bournemouth in 1934, he had already experienced many levels of football. He was an England schoolboy international in 1923, as brilliant displays for Lambton district brought him caps against Scotland and Wales. He became a professional with Sunderland and Middlesborough, without making a League appearance. Next came a move to Southport, but his career really took off when he joined Manchester City from the latter club in March 1928.

In his first season he helped City win promotion to Division One and won Lancashire Senior Cup and Manchester Senior Cup winner's medals. He played for two more seasons in Division One and when he left Maine Road had scored 46 goals in 64 matches, a remarkably consistent record at the highest level. He moved on to Bolton Wanderers, Luton Town and then Bournemouth before reaching Reading, the transfer fee of £1,000 including £200 from the Reading Football Supporters' Club.

That was in November 1934 and he made an immediate impression, scoring a hat-trick on his debut in a 5-2 away win against Aldershot. He made an impression of a different kind on (appropriately enough) Boxing Day 1934, when he punched a Millwall defender during a goalmouth tussle. The visiting player was carried off unconscious and Tait became the first Reading player to be sent off in a Football League game.

But that was Tait's style. Tough, and uncompromising, his dashing play made him a great favourite with the supporters. He headed the scoring lists in his first four seasons with Reading and when the directors put him on the transfer list at the end of the 1937/38 campaign, the crowd protested so strongly that the board changed their minds.

He remained for just one more season, which enabled him to win a Division Three (South) Cup winner's medal, as Reading beat Bristol City 6-2 on aggregate in the final. Then, despite more protests from the supporters, he moved to the South-West and Torquay United. However, his career as a combative centre forward had taken its toll, his accumulation of injuries meant that he was unable to add to his tally of appearances. He had served nine clubs, made a total of 324 Football League appearances and scored 190 goals. He died in Northwich in April 1976.

	First Team Appearances	Goals
Football League	207	24
FA Cup	13	3
FL Cup	12	1
Other	16	1
TOTAL	248	29

Scott Taylor was born in Portsmouth but his family soon moved to Bracknell, where he attended The Pines Junior School. He captained the Bracknell Primary Schools team, in which Adrian Williams also played, during the 1981/82 season, then progressed to play for East Berks and Berkshire Schools.

He joined Reading's Youth Training Scheme in 1987 and spent two years combining being coached with the mundane duties that young apprentices have to perform, such as sweeping the terraces and cleaning the senior professionals' boots. But he was making his mark in the Allied Counties and South East Counties teams and also earning an occasional outing in the Football Combination side.

Scott signed as a professional player in 1989, by which time he had already made 3 substitute appearances for the first team, and he became a regular in the line-up in 1989/90. He was competing against more experienced players for a midfield berth, but young Scott's ability to take players on and his close dribbling skills made him popular. In his six seasons with Reading he wore every outfield shirt number for the first team except the number five, a sign of his versatility. He even replaced goalkeeper Danny Honey in a reserve game against Ipswich Town after Honey had been sent off and made a number of unorthodox but effective saves – he explained afterwards that he had volunteered to go in goal because he was suffering from influenza and could not run about too much.

He was at his most subtle and energetic during the Division Two Championship of 1993/94, when he scored a string of superb individual goals as well as creating for the front players. He starred in Reading's run to the Division One play-off in 1994/95 as well and his final game for the Royals was the Wembley defeat by Bolton Wanderers.

The team began to break up after that match and Taylor was transferred to Leicester City for £500,000 in July 1995. He gained a Football League Cup winner's medal with Leicester in 1997, but suffered a serious knee injury which sidelined him for over a year. He was granted a free transfer, but Colin Lee, his former coach at Reading and by now manager of Wolverhampton Wanderers, took him to Molineux. Taylor recovered sufficiently and regained form to play a number of first team matches for Wolves during the 1999/2000 season.

Pat Terry
Centre forward, 1964-1967

	First Team Appearances	Goals
Football League	99	42
FA Cup	6	4
FL Cup	11	6
Other	0	0
TOTAL	116	52

Pat Terry was one of a number of journeymen centre forwards who proliferated during the 1950s and 1960s, moving from club to club at regular intervals. They showed no especial loyalty to any one team, but just got on with their job of scoring goals. Terry was typical of this breed. He had started with Charlton Athletic in 1954, then moved on to Newport County, Swansea Town, Gillingham, Northampton Town and finally Millwall, from whom he was transferred to Reading for £2,000 in August 1964. At that price, manager Roy Bentley had found a bargain. Terry stayed with Reading for almost three seasons, longer than he had spent with any of his previous teams, and averaged almost a goal every other game.

His style was direct and uncomplicated. He liked to bash his way through opposing defences and his aggression led to several hearings before the FA's Disciplinary Committee. It was not confined to the field either, as he once laid out a Millwall fan who abused him as he left the Elm Park pitch following a 1-1 draw at Reading.

Terry could certainly play, although his footwork was never in the same class as his heading. He was not particularly tall, but had the knack of timing his jump so that he appeared to hang in the air before meeting a cross with a bullet-like header. It was calculated that two-thirds of his goals came from his head – a real tribute to his aerial power and marksmanship.

Reading remained a mid-table side throughout his stay and in February 1967 he was sold to Swindon Town for £8,500 in another astute piece of business by Bentley. Terry ended his League career with Brentford in 1969, having totalled 227 goals in 494 Football League matches, a more than respectable return for a player who could truly be described as one of the old-fashioned type of centre forwards, whose style was more broadsword than rapier.

In his late thirties he turned out for Hillingdon Borough and Folkestone Town of the Southern League. He was also working as a London taxi driver in the Heathrow Airport area, a job he still does in the new millennium, even though he is now approaching seventy.

	First Team Appearances	Goals
Football League	203	23
FA Cup	16	3
FL Cup	15	1
Other	1	0
TOTAL	235	27

Barry Wagstaff had played alongside his older brother Tony for Sheffield United in the First Division from 1964 to 1969 before the pair joined Reading for a combined fee of £17,500. Although never quite certain of a regular first team berth at Bramall Lane, he, like Tony, added class and guile to a Reading side which was being introduced to a sophisticated style of play by new manager Jack Mansell.

He slotted straight into the side in midfield and soon demonstrated an almost languid and deceptively casual approach to the game. Never flustered or seemingly rushed, he had the unusual knack of winning the ball from an opponent with a sliding tackle from the side. His timing was immaculate and he scored some vital goals too. One of his best came with an inch perfect lob over the goalkeeper in an FA Cup tie against Arsenal in 1972. In the previous round he had scored for both teams as Reading best the amateurs of Blyth Spartans 6-1.

In fact Barry scored more goals during his time with Reading than did Tony, who played a similar amount of games yet was used in a more advanced role. Barry's reading of the game was so accurate that he was also used in the back four on occasions by Mansell's successor, Charlie Hurley, and

again he used his brain to make up for any deficiencies in pace. Barry enjoyed several spells as club captain and there were allegations of nepotism as brother Tony struggled to maintain a place in the team. However, Barry continued to put in one outstanding display after another, always appearing to play well within himself. Even in the muddiest conditions he would often leave the pitch with a clean kit, a sign of his experience and composure.

Whilst Tony left for Cheltenham Town and the Southern League in 1974, Barry stayed for one more season before returning to Yorkshire to sign for Rotherham United, where he played 45 League games and scored once. By the time he left that club he had completed a total of 419 appearances in the Football League and scored 29 goals. In recent seasons he has been working as a part-time coach at Barnsley's Centre of Excellence.

Johnny Walker
Right-back, 1957-1965

	First Team Appearances	Goals
Football League	287	24
FA Cup	21	2
FL Cup	4	1
Other	6	0
TOTAL	318	27

Veteran professionals who drop down the divisions towards the end of their careers rarely make more than a brief impact on their new club. Their name and reputation may well impress directors, but most are looking to wind down before they retire. This was not the case, however, with Johnny Walker, who had played First Division football with Wolverhampton Wanderers before moving to Southampton, then aged twenty-nine, joining Reading in 1957. Not only did he play over 300 first team games for the club, but he also proved to be one of the most charismatic and inspirational skippers Reading has ever had.

At his previous clubs Walker had played either inside right or inside left, but he retained this role for only his first season at Elm Park. He was moved subsequently to outside right, wing-half, then eventually to right-back, a position he made his own throughout the early 1960s. In that berth he could use his experience and ability to read the game to fullest advantage,

using his brain to save his legs. He could also direct and organize his players and his stentorian cry of 'Steady!' encouraged many a younger colleague to rescue a dangerous situation.

Fourteen of his 27 goals came from the penalty spot, where he was the epitome of coolness. But his rather haggard appearance got him into trouble at times and before an away game at Wrexham, some of his team told the gateman that Walker was an elderly supporter who was trying to bluff his way into the ground. Walker, who had removed his false teeth, acted the part too well, and it was nearing kick-off time before the intervention of a Reading director confirmed Walker's identity and persuaded the official to admit him.

Well-known as one of football's great characters, he was given a free transfer by Reading in the summer of 1965 and played part-time for Amersham Town. In one of his first games he told the referee, 'You'll have to excuse me for getting caught offside so often – I'm a bit quick for this class of football!'

Walker returned to Reading to play for Tilehurst in the Reading & District League then came back to Elm Park to assist the running of the reserve and youth teams part-time. By now he worked for the Post Office, but still found time to attend players' reunions at Wolves, Southampton and Reading, the three clubs he had graced with his elegant style of play.

Jimmy Wallbanks
Right-back, 1938-1947

	First Team Appearances	Goals
Football League	48	1
FA Cup	7	0
FL Cup	0	0
Other	3	0
TOTAL	58	1

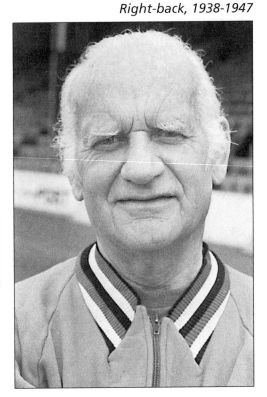

One of five brothers who all became professional footballers, Jimmy Wallbanks began his career with the Northern League side Annfield Plain, then moved into the Football League with Barnsley. He also played in pre-war football for Norwich City, Northampton Town and Wigan Athletic before joining Millwall in 1934. It was with the London club that he achieved his greatest recognition as a player. He was converted from wing-half to centre half and played there for the Millwall team which reached the semi-final of the FA Cup in 1936/37, the first Division Three team to do so. He won a Division Three (South) Championship medal with Millwall the following season, but in October 1938 was transferred to Reading, being described as a 'dapper little stopper'.

At Elm Park he was converted to right-back, but played for only one season before his career was halted by the Second World War. He played wartime football for Reading and other southern clubs, but his best years were over by the time hostilities ceased. He returned to Reading, for one more season before becoming Carlisle United's trainer, under legend Bill Shankly.

In 1951 he returned to Millwall, having qualified as a physiotherapist, and stayed until 1953. Then it was back to Reading for the third time, to combine the roles of trainer and physiotherapist for over twenty-five years. He was greatly respected and much liked by the players he treated, even though some of them gave him the affectionate nickname of 'Jimmy the Germ'. After the sacking of Jack Mansell, he became caretaker-manager for eleven matches, during which Reading won eight games before Charlie Hurley took over and Wallbanks returned to being physiotherapist.

Jimmy holds a unique Football League record. In a game at Workington on 8 November 1974, he was booked for coming onto the field without permission to treat an injured player. Thus, at the age of sixty-five, he became the oldest person ever to be cautioned in a League game.

Maurice Evans took over the job the following season, but Jimmy remained as treatment room physiotherapist and had a successful testimonial match against Queens Park Rangers in 1975. He died, aged seventy in October 1979, the day after he had been at his station for the home game against Bury. On the day of his funeral at Saint Mark's church, the Elm Park flag was flown at half-mast to mark the passing of a gentleman who had dedicated his life to Reading FC for almost forty years.

Dougie Webb

Inside left, 1956-1967

	First Team Appearances	Goals
Football League	180	81
FA Cup	12	9
FL Cup	9	2
Other	3	1
TOTAL	204	93

One of the most loyal employees a football club could ever wish to have, Douggie Webb joined Reading as an amateur straight from school and signed professional forms in 1956. He played for the club for thirteen seasons and even when his time at Elm Park was interrupted by National Service at RAF Uxbridge, he still travelled home at weekends to appear in first team or reserve games. Webb also represented the RAF and Combined Services on numerous occasions.

With Reading he appeared mostly at inside left, though there were occasional outings at inside right or on the left wing. A short, stocky and determined forward, he never gave less than his best for his only Football League club and his sheer enthusiasm won him great popularity with the supporters.

Only six players have scored more League goals for the club, even though

Webb was never an automatic first team selection. He also holds the record for reserve team goalscoring, totalling 106 and being leading Combination scorer on five occasions. He won a Football Combination Division Two Championship medal in 1966/67.

An Achilles tendon injury ended his full-time football career, but he played non-League soccer with Cheltenham Town, Dartford, Ramsgate and as player-coach at Hungerford Town.

Douggie returned to Elm Park in 1973 to take charge of the youth team and produced many gifted young players, several of whom went on to represent the club at first team level. He had the knack of getting the best out of them, but changed direction again in 1979/80 when he spent a year as the club's physiotherapist. He returned to a part-time involvement as manager of the reserve team for two more seasons before ending his connection with Reading FC in 1982.

The family association with the club continued, however. Webb's wife Joan worked in the commercial department for many years. His son Neil joined as an apprentice in 1979, before eventually playing for England.

Neil Webb

Midfielder, 1979-1982

	First Team Appearances	Goals
Football League	72	22
FA Cup	2	0
FL Cup	4	0
Other	3	0
TOTAL	81	22

The son of respected Reading player Douggie Webb, Neil Webb was destined for great things from the time he became the youngest captain of the Reading Primary Schools XI. He played regularly for Reading Reserves whilst a fifteen year old at Little Heath School and became an apprentice at Elm Park at sixteen. He was substitute for the first team within weeks and made his League debut at Mansfield on 16 February 1980. He became Reading's youngest League goalscorer in a 4-1 win over Swindon on 30 August 1980 and soon won a regular place in the team as a goalscoring midfielder.

He was a deadly penalty taker too, but it was his outstanding passing ability that earned him selection for the England Youth team. He was capped 10 times whilst with Reading, completing a hat-trick against Egypt despite playing at full-back.

His potential was studied by bigger clubs and he moved, first to Portsmouth in July 1982 for £87,500, then to Nottingham Forest in June 1985 for £250,000, with Reading receiving a third of the profit on that deal.

Neil later signed for Manchester United and by now he was a regular in the England line-up. He won 26 full England caps and also played at Under 21 and B international level. He won FA Cup and League Cup winner's medals and seemed destined for the England captaincy before a serious achilles tendon injury foreshortened his career. He was one of the leading players in English football at the time this happened and he concluded his League career with brief spells at Swindon Town, Grimsby Town and Exeter City.

He had a short time as player-coach at Weymouth, played for non-League Aldershot Town and Merthyr Tydfil, but his football activities are now confined to radio and television work. He commentates for local radio on some Reading matches and is a familiar figure in the press box at the Madejski Stadium.

Neil did make a playing comeback in the 2000/2001 season, turning out for West Reading in the Reading Football League. He also makes occasional appearances for the England Veterans' XI. But his main interest is in following his sons, Luke and Josh, who are both promising players. Luke attends the Arsenal FC Academy, while Josh trains and plays with the Academy at Reading FC.

Jimmy Wheeler

Forward, 1952-1967

	First Team Appearances	Goals
Football League	405	143
FA Cup	27	15
FL Cup	8	2
Other	13	8
TOTAL	453	168

One of the most popular players ever to wear a Reading shirt, Jimmy Wheeler scored 168 first team goals between 1952 and 1966, a total which places him second only to Trevor Senior and marginally ahead of Ron Blackman in the all-time list of Reading goalscorers. That achievement is all the more remarkable in view of the fact that while they were centre forwards, Wheeler was a winger, who could play on either flank with boundless enthusiasm and pace.

He made his name in local football with the successful Huntley & Palmers FC youth team and signed for Reading as an amateur in May 1952, turning professional a year later. He played in all five forward positions for the club, though his favoured berth was on the right wing, and for eight consecutive seasons from 1956/57 to 1963/64 reached double figures. His best return was in 1960/61, when he totalled 35 goals, the fifth highest in the club's history. The word 'mercurial' might have been invented for him, for he was a gallant chaser of passes played down either touchline and he could cut in to fire shots to the far post, meet crosses arriving from the opposite flank and out jump taller defenders to head home centres. His enthusiasm and spirit infected the players around him and he began to assist manager Roy Bentley with coaching duties towards the end of his playing career. A broken leg sustained at Barnsley in 1964 ended his career as a marauding front player, but he recovered from that injury to regain his place in the first team as a wily full-back. From that position he also captained the reserves to the Football Combination Division Two Championship in 1965/66 and after the deciding game, a 1-1 draw at home to Bournemouth Reserves, was chaired from the pitch. In the same season he was elected by fans as the club's Player of the Year, a singular distinction for a reserve team member.

His qualities as a coach, motivator and organiser led him to managership of Bradford City in 1968. In his first season he led them to promotion from Division Four and two memorable cup games against Tottenham Hotspur. He could not sustain the momentum, however, and two years later returned south to run a pub in Sandhurst.

Any all-time Reading XI would include Wheeler, for his scoring ability and volume of crosses, and his personality, which never failed to lift other members of the team. Surprisingly his only representative appearance came with selection for the Third Division (South) against the Third Division (North) in 1955/56.

The Reading team which played at Coventry City on 16 December 1962 included, from left to right, back row: Spiers, Goodall, Meeson, High, Evans. Front row: Wheeler, Whitehouse, Walker (captain), Lacey, Webb, Allen.

Jimmy Wheeler holds the Football Combination Division Two Championship Shield, which Reading won in 1965/66. Wheeler captained the reserve team from left-back, and the side regularly attracted attendances of several thousand to its home games at Elm Park.

Mark White

Utility player, 1977-1988

	First Team Appearances	Goals
Football League	278	11
FA Cup	13	1
FL Cup	23	1
Other	6	0
TOTAL	320	13

Slamming a waist-high volley past your own goalkeeper from thirty yards in one of your first home matches is hardly the way to endear yourself to the South Bank diehards. Young Mark White survived this to become one of the most popular and effective players at Elm Park and his career spanned the 1978/79 and 1985/86 championships.

Mark came to Reading on trial after being released by his home town club Sheffield United and was signed as a professional by Maurice Evans in the spring of 1977. He made his debut against Grimsby Town on 12 November 1977, forming a tight centre-back partnership with Steve Hetzke as Reading won 1-0. As a cultured defender, he found his best position to be left-back and during the Fourth Division Championship campaign of 1978/79 played in all 59 League and cup matches. This set a club record, which he shared with fellow defenders Steve Death and Martin Hicks.

The next few seasons saw him fall victim to a string of injuries that restricted his progress, but by the time Ian Branfoot had taken over as manager in January 1984, he had re-established himself in the team as a probing midfielder, able to combine sound defensive technique with an eye for a penetrating, killer pass. His goals were well-spaced but invariably spectacular. None more so than the incredible kamikaze-style diving header which secured a last minute 3-2 win over Bristol Rovers in January 1985, or his strike against York City on 27 April 1985 in a 1-2 home defeat: White netted after a precisely timed 12.96 seconds, thus recording the fastest goal ever scored by a Reading player.

In 1985/86 he scored the winning goals at Rotherham and Doncaster as Reading won their first thirteen games of the season on the way to the Division Three title and won his second championship medal. He spent two years in Division Two with the club, but injuries again restricted his appearances and he left Elm Park after enjoying a well-attended testimonial match against Chelsea in 1988.

He flew out to South Africa to prolong his career with Cape Town Spurs before returning to Reading and qualifying as a chartered physiotherapist, an occupation he still pursues in local hospitals.

	First Team Appearances	Goals
Football League	185	0
FA Cup	16	0
FL Cup	0	0
Other	12	0
TOTAL	213	0

Even by the standards of the 1930s, Percy Whittaker was on the small side for a goalkeeper. He was 5 feet 8 inches tall and weighed in at under eleven stone. He had played for Grantham before attracting the attention of Wolverhampton Wanderers who signed him in 1930 and with whom he spent three seasons. He made only 11 first team appearances for the Molineux club: 6 of them in Division Two and 5 in the FA Cup.

Nevertheless, his fearless displays between the posts had been recognised by Joe Smith, the Reading manager at the time, and when Whittaker was given a free transfer by Wolves in the summer of 1933, Smith was quick to sign him for Reading. Although Whittaker became first choice at Elm Park, replacing the veteran Dick Mellors as custodian, he never completed a full season of appearances in the Football League. Nobody doubted his ability or consistency, but his bravery –he frequently dived amongst a mass of bodies in the Reading penalty area to smother the ball – brought him a succession of injuries. In particular, a serious knee injury midway through the 1934/35 season restricted him to just 19 League games and many thought this cost Reading promotion as they finished runners-up to Charlton Athletic. In that same season he kept goal against Arsenal in the FA Cup, despite his injury, and was praised by both teams for his plucky performance as Reading were narrowly beaten by a Cliff Bastin goal.

Whittaker was considered by many to be the best goalkeeper among the Third Division clubs, but his only tangible reward came as he kept goal in both legs of the Third Division (South) Cup final, in which Reading defeated Bristol City 6-2 on aggregate in 1938.

He was released by Reading in 1939 and became a member of the training staff at the Reading Greyhound Stadium in Oxford Road. He had previously owned greyhounds, which ran at the track, but rumours which claimed that his dogs had priority over injured players on the Elm Park treatment table were strongly denied! Percy Whittaker also found time for some private life away from football whilst with Reading, for during his stay at Elm Perk he met and married the stepdaughter of Joe Smith, the manager.

Stan Wicks
Left-back, 1949-1954

	First Team Appearances	Goals
Football League	170	1
FA Cup	12	0
FL Cup	0	0
Other	0	0
TOTAL	182	1

Stan Wicks was born in Reading and had a fine career in schoolboy and youth football, which culminated in him helping the Berks & Bucks FA team to win the FA County Youth Championship in 1946. He was playing local football for the Castle Street Institute FC when he signed for Reading in 1949 and, after a handful of games for the reserves, forced his way into the first team at left-back.

He stayed in the club for the next four seasons, appearing mostly in the number three shirt, though he also performed with distinction at right-back and centre half. His imposing stature – he stood 6 feet 3 inches tall and weighed fourteen stone – enabled him to be a linchpin in the Reading rearguard as he could stretch out seemingly telescopic legs to win tackles and make lengthy clearances.

During his time at Elm Park, Reading twice went close to promotion under manager Ted Drake, and Stan's ability was recognised by selection for England B versus France B, and for the FA XI against Cambridge University.

When Drake became Chelsea manager, he remembered Stan's potential and in January 1954 signed him for the London club for £13,000. Wicks took a while to establish himself in the Chelsea first team, but eventually took over from Ron Greenwood and won a Football League Division One championship medal in 1954/55. He earned further representative honours for the Football League before a serious knee injury ended his playing days.

He returned to his home town to join the family carpet business and often attended matches at Elm Park in support of his former club. Sadly he contracted cancer and died in 1983, aged just fifty-four.

Although Stan's Reading career was a reltively brief one, he would be yet another strong contender for a place in an All-Time Reading XI. Not only was he a classy defender in the lower reaches of the Football League, he had also shown that he could hold his own at the highest level. But for that injured knee, he might have progressed onto even higher things.

Arthur Wilkie
Goalkeeper, 1961-1968

	First Team Appearances	Goals
Football League	169	2
FA Cup	11	0
FL Cup	8	0
Other	0	0
TOTAL	**188**	**2**

Although Arthur Wilkie kept goal for Reading's first team in almost 200 League and cup games, it is as a goalscorer that he is most frequently remembered by collectors of curious football statistics.

On 31 August 1962, he was injured whilst making a save for Reading in a home game against Halifax Town. In those pre-substitute days it was traditional for any injured player to take up a winger's position to avoid further injury. Thus Wilkie moved onto an outfield flanking position whilst Maurice Evans took over as emergency goalkeeper.

Reading won the League match 4-2 and Wilkie, who had often played outfield in six-a-side and practice games, netted two of the Reading goals, thus setting a record for a goalkeeper in a first class game. Arthur was later given a brief run as a forward in the Football Combination and again got amongst the goals, but never started a first team match as anything other than a 'keeper.

He had joined the Elm Park groundstaff in November 1958, and made his League debut for Reading on 30 September 1961. He shared the goalkeeping duties with Mike Dixon for most of the decade and was often rumoured to be the target of bigger clubs. Burnley especially noticed him after his superb displays against them in the FA Cup tie and replay of 1965, but he remained with his only Football League club until 1968.

Agile, brave and a safe handler of crosses, he experienced a bad back injury towards the end of his time with Reading. His nemesis came in a 1-5 defeat at Swindon, when he was unable to reproduce his former ability. Wilkie left the club in the summer of 1968 and signed for Chelmsford City of the Southern League. After a couple of seasons with that club, he returned nearer home when he linked up with Basingstoke Town, whom he helped to reach the FA Cup first round in 1971/72, which was also their first season in the Southern League.

Arthur later played local League football in Reading as a centre forward for Cotswold. He was a table tennis player of some repute as well, but severed all his ties with the Reading area when he emigrated to New Zealand.

Adrian Williams

Utility player, 1988-1996, 1999-present

	First Team Appearances	Goals
Football League	211	15
FA Cup	16	2
FL Cup	17	2
Other	15	2
TOTAL	259	21

One of a cluster of young players to emerge from Ian Branfoot's highly successful investment in local talent, Bracknell-born Adrian Williams made his first team debut in a 3-3 draw at Notts County on 22 October 1988. It had been a quick promotion for Williams, who had played for the South East Counties side the previous week, but he confirmed his right to higher status with a string of competent performances before the end of the season.

He made spasmodic appearances over the next three years, but fulfilled his vast potential when Mark McGhee took over as manager in May 1991. In the transitional campaign of 1991/92 he became a first team regular, but appeared in several different positions, including a spell of nine games at striker when he replaced Trevor Senior. Niggling injuries kept him out of the line-up for a while, but when he wore the number ten shirt against Wrexham on 5 March 1994, he had completed a unique achievement. He had then worn every possible first team shirt number and appeared in every position, including two appearances as emergency substitute goalkeeper. He was the only Football League player to do so and had completed this remarkable feat at the age of just twenty-two.

He won a Division Two Championship medal with Reading in that season of 1993/94 and international recognition followed. He was selected for Wales against Estonia in a summer friendly match, the first of 7 caps he was to win for his country whilst with Reading. The following season he was the veritable rock at the heart of the Reading defence and scored the winner against Charlton which ensured a play-off place He also scored in the play-off final at Wembley, but it was not enough to secure Premiership football and a year later he was transferred to Wolverhampton Wanderers for £1,000,000. He was reunited there with Mark McGhee and former Reading coach Colin Lee, but more injuries meant that he did not become a permanent feature in the Wolves team, which almost secured a place in the Premiership.

Adrian returned to Reading on loan from Wolves in February 2000 to shore up the defence as the team struggled to pull away from the foot of Division Two. In a fifteen game run he showed that he had lost none of his poise or popularity. So dominant was he that Royals' supporters hoped the move would be permanent. Indeed, he rejoined Reading on a free transfer before the start of the 2000/01 season.

Bobby Williams
Forward, 1969-1971

	First Team Appearances	Goals
Football League	65	21
FA Cup	5	1
FL Cup	1	0
Other	1	0
TOTAL	72	22

The nickname of 'Shadow' fitted Bobby Williams perfectly. As a player he had the knack of ghosting in on the blindside of defenders to score goals and as youth team coach, a position he held at Reading for twenty-five years, he was unobtrusively effective in preparing and producing first team players.

His playing career began with Bristol City, his home town club, for whom he made his League debut on 18 April 1959. He represented the FA Youth XI, won Gloucestershire Senior Cup medals, and was a member of the City team which won promotion from Division Three in 1964/65. He totalled 76 goals in 188 Football League appearances before joining Rotherham United then Bristol Rovers, though he never enjoyed the same recognition at the latter clubs.

Jack Mansell brought Bobby to Reading in August 1969 and he became part of the small but sophisticated forward line which profited from the manager's emphasis on attacking football. A total of 87 League goals earned Reading entry to the Watney Cup and a proud moment came when Bobby captained Reading against Manchester United in that competition. The following season of 1970/71 was a disastrous one, as Reading were relegated to Division Four in the club's centenary year and he was one of six players given free transfers in the summer.

His goalscoring and goalmaking ratio at Reading remained high, and he had little difficulty in finding another club, though he had to travel abroad. He signed for ASO Ostend of Belgium, with Denis Allen and Roger Smee, but after one season transferred to Weymouth of the Southern League. A serious car accident finished his playing career and he returned to Elm Park to manage the reserve and youth teams.

William's value to Reading FC was incalculable during his spell in charge of the youths. He had the ability to recruit and motivate youngsters, besides teaching the basics of the game, and more than forty players progressed through the South Eastern Counties and Allied Counties sides to eventually reach first team level. Notable amongst these were Neil Webb, Sanchez, Lovell, Adrian Williams and Scott Taylor. Bobby still enjoyed playing in charity and friendly games, although his only appearance for Beetle & Wedge FC resulted in a hip replacement operation! One of the best known and most popular figures around the Madejski Stadium, Williams still uses his vast experience of the game as a scout for the club.

Jerry Williams
Utility player, 1976-1988

	First Team Appearances	Goals
Football League	309	17
FA Cup	14	0
FL Cup	15	1
Other	19	0
TOTAL	357	18

The football career of Jerry Williams has come full circle by 2000. He was spotted by coach Maurice Evans whilst playing junior football in Didcot and joined Reading in 1976, aged sixteen. He starred in the junior, youth and reserve teams before making his debut as a substitute against Bury on 26 February 1977. Reading were beaten 3-1 and manager Charlie Hurley resigned at half-time.

Young Jerry recovered from that shock to make irregular appearances for the first team over the next four seasons as a front player, as Evans kept faith with his protege. However, it was a switch of position to right-back midway through the 1980/81 campaign that saw him gain a permanent place in the side and he was elected Player of the Year in 1981/82. He was a steady, dependable and dogged defender, but he also used his asset of good pace to make exciting runs forward.

He kept his place as Ian Branfoot took over the team and won a Division Three

Championship medal in 1985/86. He headed the first goal of the record-breaking run in 1-0 victory over Blackpool, but played the whole of the season on a weekly contract after failing to agree terms with the club. Neither was he granted the testimonial he had been promised with Reading, but he remained loyal and played for the Royals for two more seasons as the club struggled to survive in Division Two. He won another medal on 27 March 1983, when he was used as a late substitute in the 4-1 Simod Cup final victory over Luton Town at Wembley.

By the time he left he had starred at full-back, in midfield and up front, proving to be one of the best local discoveries unearthed by the club. In the summer of 1988 he moved to Gillingham as a player-exchange for Karl Elsey. He spent a year there, then two at Aldershot before that club left the Football League.

1991 saw Jerry playing as a part-timer for Windsor & Eton FC, while working as an agent for the Liverpool & Victoria Friendly Society. He is now a self-employed financial adviser with Premier Financial Management. Football however remains his first love and although he no longer plays, he has been manager of the Didcot Boys team for the last three seasons. His sons, Luke and Jordan, both play for the club and Jerry's wife, Paula, acts as secretary. The family live in Didcot, where he has returned to his footballing roots.

Steve Wood

Centre-back, 1979-1987

	First Team Appearances	Goals
Football League	219	9
FA Cup	15	0
FL Cup	10	0
Other	7	0
TOTAL	251	9

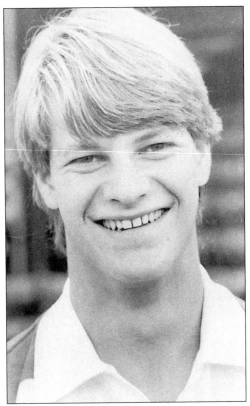

Born in Bracknell in 1963, Steve Wood originally signed for Arsenal as an associate schoolboy, after impressing with his performances for the East Berks and Berkshire Schools teams. Opportunities were limited at Highbury, however, and he came to Reading as an apprentice in 1979. His displays in the South East Counties team were outstanding and he was quickly promoted to the Football Combination side. He understudied first team regular Steve Hetzke briefly and when Hetzke was injured made his first team debut against Southend United on 25 February 1980 – just three weeks past his seventeenth birthday.

Wood gave a consummate performance against an experienced striker and would have enjoyed a longer run in the side but for a serious knee injury which hampered his career for several months. However, he became first choice at centre-back from the start of the 1981/82 season and was a member of the team which gained promotion to Division Three in 1983/84. He did not miss a game in either 1984/85 or 1985/86 and his greatest success at Elm Park came in the latter campaign, when he won a Division Three Championship medal. That was the season when Reading equalled a Football League record by winning their first eleven games and it was Wood's goal that did the trick, as he volleyed home in the 1-0 victory over Bolton Wanderers. He scored other vital goals that year too, but his main contribution to the team was as a central defender who could be described as no-nonsense, yet classy. He had pace, timing, strength and excellent range of passes out of defence.

He was popular with supporters too, always willing to attend functions and presentations, and it was a big loss to Reading FC when, having played for just one season in Division Two, he was sold to Millwall for £60,000. He remained with the London club for four years, winning a Division Two Championship medal in 1987/88, then signed for Southampton for a fee of £450,000 in October 1991. He was at the Dell for three more seasons before winding down his career with Oxford United then Woking.

At the conclusion of his playing career he set up a chain of soccer schools at Farnham and he is also a partner in a sports agency. He still shows flashes of his undoubted skill in ex-Reading XI charity games.

Tommy Youlden

Central defender, 1972-1977

	First Team Appearances	Goals
Football League	163	3
FA Cup	6	0
FL Cup	14	0
Other	0	0
TOTAL	183	3

An England schoolboy international who played against Northern Ireland Schools at Elm Park in 1964, Tommy Youlden began his professional career at Arsenal, where he was a member of the Gunners' FA Youth Cup winning team.

First team opportunities at Highbury were limited, so he moved to Portsmouth . He made 82 Football League appearances for the South Coast club at centre half.

In the summer of 1972 he was signed by Charlie Hurley – always an excellent judge of a defender – for £10,000, and proved to be another of the Reading manager's bargain buys.

Youlden immediately formed a solid, uncompromising central defensive partnership with skipper John Hulme and remained an automatic first choice throughout his five years at Elm Park. He only ever lost his place through injury and contributed significantly to the club's promotion from Division Four in the 1975/76 season.

He was a classy, composed but not overly adventurous player, and scored just three goals during his time with the Royals. He is perhaps best remembered for a bizarre incident in a game against Rochdale on the first day of the promotion season. In the first half he took a free kick from outside the penalty area and, although his drive thudded into the side netting, the referee awarded a goal as the ball bounced back onto the pitch. He and the linesman were the only people in the ground who did not realise what had happened, but the goal stood as Reading won 2-0.

Youlden was transferred to Aldershot for the amazingly low fee of £2,500 in 1977 and made a further 118 League appearances. He then had a brief spell with Addlestone & Weybridge before retiring from the game.

Tommy took an external maths degree before becoming a maths and PE teacher. Now living in Surbiton, his current involvement in football is as one of the coaches at the Chelsea FC Academy where he trains and manages the Under 14 squad.